U.S. Department of Justice
Office of Justice Programs
Office for Victims of Crime

VICTIM IMPACT:
Listen and Learn

PARTICIPANT WORKBOOK

Innovation • Partnerships
Safer Neighborhoods

Office for Victims of Crime
OVC
"Putting Victims First"

U.S. Department of Justice
Office of Justice Programs
810 Seventh Street NW.
Washington, DC 20531

Mark Filip
Acting Attorney General

Laurie Robinson
Acting Assistant Attorney General

Joye E. Frost
Acting Director, Office for Victims of Crime

Office of Justice Programs
Innovation • Partnerships • Safer Neighborhoods
www.ojp.usdoj.gov

Office for Victims of Crime
www.ovc.gov

NCJ 224257

This product was supported by grant number 2005–VF–GX–K026, awarded by the Office for
Victims of Crime, Office of Justice Programs, U.S. Department of Justice. The opinions, findings,
and conclusions or recommendations expressed in this product are those of the contributors and do
not necessarily represent the official position or policies of the U.S. Department of Justice.

VICTIM IMPACT:
Listen and Learn

PARTICIPANT WORKBOOK

Contents

Acknowledgments

The Office for Victims of Crime (OVC), within the U.S. Department of Justice's Office of Justice Programs, awarded a cooperative agreement to the California Department of Corrections and Rehabilitation, Office of Victim and Survivor Services (OVSS), to develop a standardized victim impact curriculum for corrections. The 18-month project began on October 1, 2005.

The project team included Project Director Sharon English, Dr. Kevin "Kip" Lowe, and OVSS staff members Jill Weston and Suzanne Neuhaus. Contracted consultants were Drs. Mario Gaboury and Christopher Sedelmaier from the University of New Haven and national expert Anne Seymour. Frankie Lemus of The Change Companies® served as the curriculum manager.

State pilot sites were California, Ohio, Tennessee, and Virginia. The project team is indebted to state coordinators Michael Davis in Ohio, Sheryl DeMott in Tennessee, and Wendy Lohr-Hopp in Virginia. The team also thanks corrections directors James Tilton, Gene Johnson, George Little, and Terry Collins for their willingness to host this project in their facilities.

An active and insightful 15-member advisory board, which included 12 crime victims or survivors of crime, guided the curriculum development. Lists of the board and the pilot site locations are included in appendixes E and F.

The curriculum was finalized with considerable input from the offenders who participated in the classes, the instructors, and the victim speakers whose willingness and courage ensured that the materials are victim centered. We are grateful for their time and dedication. The instructors were—

California: Laura Bowman, Chris Wittek, Felicia Jones

Ohio: John Culp, Roxanne Swogger, Vicki Knapp, Eldie Antenuce, Bette Erwin, Martha Moore, Tammy Nevil, Jacque Sauer, Mindy Rosengarten, Debbie Hall, Tami Perez

Tennessee: Dr. Jennie Jobe, Ricky Bunch, Dr. Sharon Taylor

Virginia: Cynthia Smith, Cate Kaufmann

The project team appreciates the assistance provided by OVC grant monitor Kim Kelberg for her support, guidance, and advocacy for this important program. Former OVC Director John Gillis, one of the first California Impact of Crime on Victims class speakers in the 1980s, has been a dedicated voice on behalf of victims' rights and we thank him for his support of innovative programs.

The statistics and trends used throughout this workbook were gathered from the 2006 and 2007 OVC Crime Victimization in the United States Statistical Overviews, available in the *National Crime Victims' Rights Week Resource Guide*, and the 2005 and 2006 Federal Bureau of Investigation's Uniform Crime Index.

Unit 1. Getting Started

Welcome to Victim Impact: Listen and Learn. This program helps you to learn about the impact of crime on victims. You will have opportunities to learn information and skills that benefit you. The program challenges you to begin to focus on other people . . . people you have harmed. This is not a class about sentencing laws or offender rights. The focus is on victims. Although you may already think about the people that you have victimized, you may not know what it feels like to be victimized yourself. During this program, you will participate in activities, watch videos, and hear victims speak. You will see and hear directly from victims about how their lives have changed.

This program consists of 13 units, built around 10 core crime topics: property crime, assault, robbery, hate and bias, gang violence, sexual assault, child abuse and neglect, domestic violence, drunk and impaired driving, and homicide. Each unit will take approximately 2.5 hours to complete. In this first session, I will explain what the program is all about and go over the program objectives and ground rules for participating. I'll have you sign the class contract and take a pre-test, which will be administered again at the end of the program. The second class will introduce the concept of victim impact through class discussion and a series of group activities. During the remaining weeks, we will cover the 10 core crime topics.

Here are some thoughts and feelings you may be experiencing:

I don't know how my actions hurt someone.

I'm the victim, I got caught.

It was a victimless crime.

These are my thoughts and feelings about starting this program:

_____

_____

_____

_____

_____

_____

_____

You are not the first person to wonder, "What will I learn in this class?" After taking the class, many offenders have the attitude, "This is the most important program I have completed. What can I do now?" As you participate in this class, you too may change your thinking about crime and victimization. This class is just the start. If you find yourself asking, "What now?" other programs are available that handle the following issues:

- Restitution
- Community service
- Restorative justice
- Counseling
- Life skills
- Substance abuse
- Parenting

This is what I hope to gain from this class:

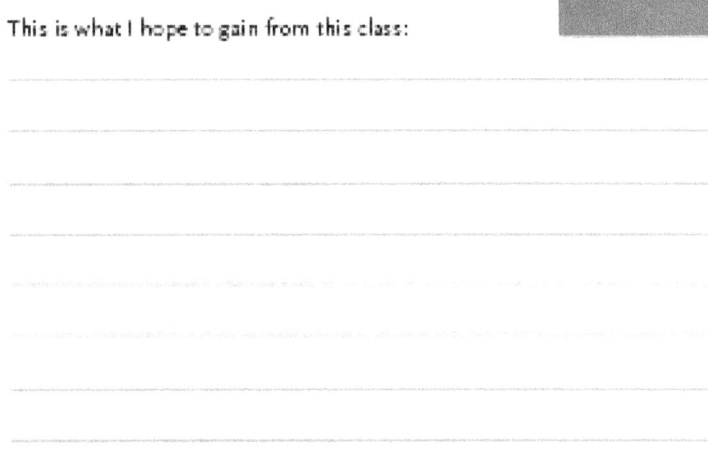

_____

_____

_____

_____

_____

_____

Offenders need to know what they interrupted in my life.

—Cheryl Ward-Kaiser
homicide/robbery survivor

Unit 2: Introduction to Victim Impact

Before we get into the core crime units, we will define who is a victim and talk about victims' rights. Who do you think has more rights under the criminal justice system: victims or offenders?

As a group, we will discuss and list the rights of each group.

- Did anything surprise you about these lists?
- How do you think a victim would feel about these lists?
- What rights do you think victims would like to add?
- What have you learned from this activity?

Core Victim Rights: There are several general core rights to which victims are entitled. These include—

- Information/referral: The right to information about the offender, the case proceedings, and the offender's disposition. The right to be referred to people and agencies that can assist them.
- Notification: The right to receive notice of offender status such as arrest, release on bail, and/or release to parole.
- Safety: The right to protection beginning at the crime scene and continuing through the offender's release on parole.
- Restitution/compensation: The right to seek restitution directly from the offender for losses resulting from the crime. In addition, victims have the right to apply to their respective State Victim Compensation Fund for financial assistance.
- Participation: The right to attend certain proceedings and/or submit a victim impact statement.

Defining Who Is a Victim

During this program, the term "crime victim" will stand for any person or persons, group, business, or organization that has been harmed and/or injured as a result of criminal activity. A "ripple effect" describes how the impact of crime can spread beyond the immediate victim throughout his or her family, friends, and community.

Types of victims:

Primary, immediate, or direct victims have been directly harmed by an offender. Some victims call themselves survivors.

Survivors are usually considered family and close friends of a homicide victim. Some survivors call themselves victims.

Secondary victims or covictims have a close relationship with the victim.

Areas of Impact: How Are People Harmed?

Being victimized is a shocking experience for people. Regardless of the type of crime, victims may experience intense fear, helplessness, or horror. Some may even develop posttraumatic stress disorder. Crime victims may become afraid of people who share the offender's characteristics (e.g., age, race, voice tone, clothing, body language, or distinctive features). They may react negatively to smells or noises that remind them of the crime scene. Their behavior may change toward the people around them. Symptoms may last for a short time or linger for years.

Although victims react in individual ways, there are four basic areas of impact for all victims: physical, financial, emotional, and religious/spiritual. Keep these in mind because areas of impact will be discussed in each unit.

After the Crime, Victims —

- May worry about being believed or about being blamed or second-guessed for their behavior before, during, and after the crime.
- May become upset and/or have flashbacks in reaction to certain noises, smells, times of day, or times of month that remind them of the victimization.
- May become afraid of people who share the offender's characteristics: age, race, voice tone, clothing, body language, or distinctive features.
- May spend much time filling out forms for the police, finding paperwork to give to the insurance company, making decisions about funeral arrangements, paying their bills, and caring for their distraught families.

Unit 3: Property Crime

What Is Property Crime?

The word "property" generally refers to land, buildings, or personal items such as money or cars. Property crime is the illegal taking or destroying of someone's property or land without threats or force. Auto theft, burglary, forgery, shoplifting, and larceny (theft) are examples of the illegal taking of property. Arson and vandalism are crimes that damage land or property.

Although property crimes are not defined as involving threats or force, this does not mean they are victimless crimes or "just" minor offenses. Crimes are committed against people, not against property. Even if the victim does not witness the crime, its aftermath may be frightening, life-changing, and disturbing. Offenders can cause victims significant fear or distress and can disrupt their lives by stealing a car or stereo, burglarizing a home or business, setting a building on fire, or shoplifting.

Offenders are responsible for what happens to a victim during a crime, including indirect injury to the victim. An example of indirect injury might be the victim having a heart attack in response to the crime. Property crimes can be especially difficult for older people as they may not have money or insurance to replace property and may have sentimental feelings about the stolen or damaged items.

Children may find property crime especially frightening if the crime occurs in or near the home.

When a property crime occurs, some people think that insurance companies can solve the victim's problems. The original reason for having insurance was to cover accidents, such as someone backing into a car or accidentally hitting a baseball through a neighbor's window. Today, insurance companies process many claims for stolen cars, home and auto burglaries, stolen stereo equipment, and graffiti cleanup.

Insurance companies have systems for how they pay victims and how much they pay for items. A victim may not be paid the full amount for an older TV or receive the full purchase price of a car because the item loses value over time. In addition, insurance companies require that victims pay part of the loss, called a deductible. Deductibles can range from $100 to $1,000, which is an out-of-pocket cost to the victim.

Money cannot buy my heart.

— Burglary victim, regarding the loss of sentimental items

Words To Know

- Arson
- Burglary
- Embezzlement
- Extortion
- Insurance deductible
- Irreplaceable
- Larceny/theft
- Memorabilia
- Sentimental value
- Vandalism

Property crime victims have to deal with—

- Having their privacy violated.
- Being scared to stay in their burglarized homes.
- Being scared to return to work, where the crime occurred.
- Seeing their businesses burned down.
- Waiting a long time to have their property returned.
- Cleaning up after their homes or businesses have been vandalized.
- Filling out insurance paperwork.

In the News: Property Crime Trends

Every day you can find television or newspaper stories about property crime. Take a look at the property crime trends below. Which trend is the most surprising to you?

- Property crime makes up approximately 75 percent of all crimes in the United States.

- Only a small percentage of stolen property is found or returned to victims.

- Burglary is the most common property crime.

- Property crime, regardless of the type, occurs more often to those living in rented property.

- The estimated loss for theft is between $50 and $250.

- The estimated yearly loss due to property crimes (except arson) is more than $10 billion.

- More than $4 billion is spent on locks and safes, $1.4 billion on surveillance cameras, and $49 million on guard dogs.

Examples of Property Crime

The following are definitions and examples of nine types of property crime. As you read each story, consider the impact on victims.

Burglary

Unlawful entry of a structure to commit a felony or theft.

John and Maria return home from the store and see that their front door is open. Their stereo and TV have been stolen. How do you think John and Maria feel?

_____

_____

_____

_____

Receipt of Stolen Property

Buying or receiving property that has been stolen or has been obtained through theft or extortion.

George and Damon are in a public parking lot selling stolen TVs at a discount from their van. How do you think George and Damon obtained the stolen TVs?

_____

_____

_____

_____

They are there for 20 minutes to wreck your life . . . and your sense of security.

—Burglary victim

Larceny/Theft

Unlawful taking of property from another (e.g., shoplifting, picking pockets, purse snatching, thefts from motor vehicles, thefts of motor vehicle parts and accessories, bicycle thefts).

Nine-year-old Connor is riding his bike home from school and is stopped by a group of four older kids. They tell him to get off his bike, make him drop his backpack, and then run away laughing with his backpack. How would you feel if Connor were your son or brother?

_____

_____

_____

Auto Theft

Theft or attempted theft of a motor vehicle.

Ahn and his two kids have been to a Saturday afternoon movie at a local theater. When they reach the parking lot, Ahn hears his daughter, Mila, say, "Daddy! Look! Our car is gone, and there's broken glass all over." How do you feel about what happened to Ahn and his kids?

_____

_____

_____

> *Me and my kids should not have to be afraid in our own home.*
>
> —Burglary victim

Vandalism

Willful or malicious damage or destruction of property.

Lynne volunteered to work at a high school wrestling match held at a rival school. After the meet, in the school parking lot, she noticed her tire was flat. Her tire had been punctured and the whole side of her car had been "keyed." How would you react if Lynne were your sister?

_____

_____

_____

> *I keep asking, "Why would someone do this to me? What did I do to deserve this?"*
>
> —Vandalism victim

Embezzlement

Misappropriation or misapplication of another person's money or property.

Minh and Amy are friends who both work in a coffee shop, usually during the same shift. They take turns counting the money from the cash register at the end of their shift. Every other day they put some of the money that does not belong to them directly in their pockets. Who are Minh and Amy harming by stealing money?

_____

_____

_____

Arson

Willful or malicious burning or attempting to burn another person's house, public building, motor vehicle, or other personal property.

A group of teenagers set fire to a shed using gasoline, rags, and lighters. Jackie uses the shed to store furniture and personal items. The shed and all the property inside are damaged. Who has been harmed by the teenagers' behavior?

_____

_____

_____

> *I don't understand what he was thinking, but his stupid act has ruined the lives of people he didn't even know.*
>
> —Arson victim

Extortion

Using fear of death, injury, property loss, reputation, and so forth to compel another person to deliver property or perform some act or omission.

John and Bobby, members of a local gang, go into a store and tell the owner that he has to pay them money on a weekly schedule to "protect" his business from rival gang members. They also tell him that he has to give them free alcohol. How do you think the store owner feels?

_____

_____

_____

Forgery

Making, altering, or possessing a fake copy of a document or object with the intent to deceive. Attempted forgeries are included in this category.

Mr. Singh is elderly and lives with his family because he cannot read well anymore and gets confused easily. Without anyone's permission, his nephew has been writing checks from Mr. Singh's personal checking account, signing Mr. Singh's name, and spending the money on drugs. What are the possible injuries to Mr. Singh resulting from his nephew's behavior?

_____

_____

_____

_____

 ## What Is the Impact of Property Crime?

Criminal behavior such as property crime causes a ripple effect that has a negative impact on a number of life areas. The lists below outline some examples of how property crime affects financial, physical, emotional, and religious/spiritual areas of victims' lives. Add your own examples below.

Financial

- Property loss
- Payment of insurance deductible
- _____
- _____
- _____

Physical

- Headaches
- Stress reactions
- Problems sleeping
- _____
- _____

Emotional

- Fear
- Anger
- Insecurity
- _____
- _____
- _____

Religious/Spiritual

- Questioning the goodness of others
- Questioning the right to have material possessions
- _____
- _____
- _____

Victim Impact: Listen and Learn

After viewing the OVC *Victim Impact: Listen and Learn* DVD clip about burglary, answer the following questions:

What were the financial losses?

_____

_____

How did this burglary affect Leanna and her family?

_____

_____

 ## Being Accountable for Your Crimes

Property crime has a serious financial and emotional impact on victims. Victims suffer from a loss of security in their own homes, businesses, or workplaces. Their privacy is violated. They may never regain the sense of security they once had. No one has the right to commit a property crime, regardless of the circumstances. No one has the right to harm another person.

How Can I Be Accountable for My Crimes?

> I need to figure out why I commit property crimes.
> —Joe

> I need to respect people's property. What if someone burglarized my family's home?
> —Jerome

> I scared that family by breaking into their home. I need to admit that my behavior was serious and I hurt people.
> —Tanya

> I destroyed things that were important to the victim.
> —Manny

Additional Activities

Activity A — What Is Important to You?

Someone breaks into your place and steals from you. Pick the one item that would bother you the most if someone were to steal it. You *have* to pick one.

- Your CD and DVD collection
- Your most important piece of jewelry
- Your credit cards
- Important paperwork
- $100 cash
- Your child's baby pictures

After you discuss this activity in class, write down your thoughts and feelings.

_____

_____

_____

Activity C — The Sanchez Family

Tony takes his grandparents, Mr. and Mrs. Sanchez, to cash their Social Security checks and then they rent a few movies. When they go home, they see that it has been broken into. The house is a mess. The following items have been stolen: TV, $300 from a cookie jar, and jewelry from Mrs. Sanchez's grandmother. In addition, these items have been broken or destroyed: the cookie jar, Mr. and Mrs. Sanchez's wedding picture, clothes (thrown around the bedroom), and a religious book.

What might Mr. and Mrs. Sanchez be thinking or feeling?

_____

What might Tony be thinking or feeling?

_____

What might Mr. and Mrs. Sanchez experience in the next few days?

_____

What might the emotional impact be on Mr. and Mrs. Sanchez 6 months from now?

_____

What are the irreplaceable items that were taken or destroyed?

_____

Which items will the insurance company cover?

- TV
- Money
- Religious book
- Lock on front door
- Jewelry
- Cookie jar
- Wedding picture frame
- New burglar alarm

Activity D— Elisa

Elisa makes $7 an hour working 20 hours a week in a restaurant. She is studying photography and recently bought a $500 camera with her tax refund, overtime pay, and birthday money. Someone broke into Elisa's locker at work and stole the camera. She does not have insurance.

How many hours of work will it take to replace the camera?

_____

_____

How long will it take Elisa to replace the camera?

_____

_____

Is it realistic to think that Elisa can use all of her work money to replace her camera in that time period? What other expenses may she have?

_____

_____

If the offender is charged with a crime and ordered to pay restitution, how soon will Elisa receive restitution payments for the camera?

_____

_____

Unit 4. Assault

What Is Assault?

The legal definitions of "assault" vary from state to state; however, there are two general categories:

Aggravated assault is an unlawful attack on another person for the purpose of causing severe physical injury. An assault is usually called "aggravated" when it involves a weapon that could cause serious physical harm or death. You can be convicted of aggravated assault even if the victim was not physically harmed.

Simple assault is the attempt or threat to inflict less serious physical injury without a weapon.

The number of assaults is much higher than the number of homicides in the United States. Unlike other violent crimes, assaults are committed almost equally by strangers and nonstrangers, which means that many victims know their attackers. Nearly one out of every four assaults occurs in the victim's home; at a relative's, friend's, or neighbor's home; or on the street near the victim's home. Many juvenile assault victims say the first assault they remember occurred in their homes. In these cases, the attackers generally have been family members, friends, and acquaintances.

Victims may be threatened or attacked by offenders who have guns, baseball bats, knives, or other objects used as weapons. They may also be slapped, punched, or kicked. Victims' physical injuries include broken bones, serious bruises and sprains, lost teeth, internal injuries, and loss of consciousness. Even if assault victims are not subjected to serious injuries or losses, they may suffer intense fear, threats of additional violence, and physical harm at the hands of their assailants. Assault victims often experience shock, ongoing fear, distress, or a loss of their sense of reality. They may experience flashbacks, anxiety, or an inability to concentrate. These reactions and feelings, which are common responses to a traumatic event, are referred to as posttraumatic stress disorder.

Words To Know

- Aggravated assault
- Posttraumatic stress disorder (PTSD)
- Simple assault

In the News: Assault Trends

Assault can have a devastating impact on people. Take a look at the facts about assault below. Which trend bothers you the most?

- Assault is the most common violent crime in the United States.
- About one-fourth of assaults in the United States involve a weapon. Hands, fists, and feet are the most common weapons used in assaults.
- The age group most likely to become victims of aggravated assault is 18- to 24-year-olds.

Examples of Assault

The FBI defines simple assault as an attack that does not involve a dangerous weapon and that leaves no serious injuries; aggravated assault involves both. The following are five examples of both types of assault. As you read each story, consider the impact on the victims.

Simple Assault

On the way home from the local grocery store, Margaret, age 79, was verbally threatened by two large men wearing ski masks. They did not have weapons, but they caused her extreme shock, fright, and distress. During the assault, the men wrestled her purse from her, causing Margaret to fall, but she did not require medical attention.

How would you feel if Margaret were your grandmother?

_____

_____

_____

Why did this happen to me? I didn't do anything wrong.

—Assault victim

I'm afraid that they'll come back to finish me off.

—Assault victim

Aggravated Assault

James, a parent at a youth soccer game, argued with the referee about a call. When the referee told James to "be quiet and sit down," he attacked the referee, punching him several times in the face and chest.

What were the referee's injuries?

_____

_____

_____

Albert was stabbed in the stomach when he confronted his nephew, Raul, about stealing money from him to buy drugs.

How did Raul harm his Uncle Albert?

_____

_____

_____

_____

Aggravated Assault and Hate Crime

Brent, 28, ended up in the emergency room with a collapsed lung and a concussion after he was attacked by a group of people who kicked him repeatedly and hit him with heavy sticks. His attackers targeted him because they thought he was gay.

What are your reactions to this crime?

_____

_____

_____

_____

I don't enjoy the little pleasures I once enjoyed. Life just doesn't seem the same anymore.

—Assault victim

Aggravated Assault and Gang Violence

Ming, a junior high school student, had his nose broken by gang members who hit him with baseball bats and kicked him in the face because he was wearing their gang colors.

What do you think happens to Ming after the assault?

_____

_____

_____

_____

When people look at my scars, I tell them I got into a car accident. They wouldn't be able to handle what really happened to me.

—Assault victim, regarding his injuries

What Is the Impact of Assault?

The following lists outline some examples of how simple and aggravated assault affects financial, physical, emotional, and religious/spiritual areas of victims' lives. Add your own examples below.

Financial

- Medical bills
- Insurance deductible
- _____
- _____
- _____

Physical

- Broken bones
- Cuts
- Facial disfigurement
- Fatigue
- Problems sleeping
- Loss of sight and hearing
- Brain damage
- _____
- _____
- _____

Emotional

- Fear
- Paranoia
- Anger
- Thoughts of revenge
- Vulnerability
- _____
- _____
- _____

Religious/Spiritual

- "Why Me?"
- _____
- _____
- _____

Victim Impact: Listen and Learn

After viewing the OVC *Victim Impact: Listen and Learn* DVD clip about assault, answer the following questions:

What was the physical impact?

_____

_____

_____

_____

> *What good am I now? I can't do anything without someone having to help me.*
>
> —Assault victim, regarding physical disabilities

What was the emotional impact?

_____

_____

_____

_____

Being Accountable for Your Crimes

How victims react to being assaulted varies from person to person. An assault is a violent, life-threatening crime. Even if a victim is not seriously or permanently injured, during the assault, he or she had to deal with the possibility of serious injury, death, and fears of leaving loved ones behind. This can have a great emotional impact on victims—immediately and in the long term. Victims may survive an assault, but often are changed forever. No one has the right to harm another person.

How Can I Be Accountable for My Crimes?

> *I scared that woman and her child. What if it happened to my mom and kid sister?*
>
> —William

> *Now that family has hospital bills to pay, thanks to me. I need to do my part.*
>
> —Carla

> *Not only does she have to deal with it on the inside, she's reminded everytime she looks in the mirror. I'm not proud of my actions.*
>
> —Ross

> *While I'm locked up, I will be nonviolent. When I get out, I will stay committed to nonviolent behavior.*
>
> —J.R.

How do you think the victims of these offenders would feel hearing these statements?

_____

_____

_____

_____

Additional Activity

Activity A — Assault Victim's Impact Statement

Read the following victim impact statement and write down your thoughts, feelings, and comments.

On Sunday evening, our son Adam and his friends were walking in a residential neighborhood. Five offenders approached them and blocked their path. One of the offenders pointed a gun at the victims and said, "Have you ever seen a .357 magnum?"

Two offenders pushed Adam to the ground and all five punched and kicked him repeatedly in he face. Adam put his arms up to try to protect himself. He had on a leather jacket, and they beat and kicked him so badly that the leather on the jacket had worn spots. The police were called and the offenders fled the scene but were caught after a high-speed chase. When the offenders were caught they had Adam's blood on their shoes.

We drove 3 hours to the hospital. It is extremely difficult to talk about the feelings we experienced when we first saw Adam in the hospital. Seeing your only son physically traumatized to the point where he can't open his eyes or mouth and is being given morphine to endure the pain is indescribable. Adam had a broken nose, deviated septum, shattered right cheekbone, fractures to the bones around his right eye socket, and several front teeth knocked out.

He had to have extensive facial reconstructive surgery and could not eat solid food for some time. His nose had to be rebroken a year later during a 4-hour operation because he could not breathe well. When Adam was recovering from the attack we covered the mirrors in the house because he did not want to see the visible results of the beating.

The robbery and savage attack were not spontaneous. It was a planned, calculated act, the second robbery the offenders committed that day. Because of this crime against Adam and his friends, people living in that neighborhood were afraid to walk or jog after dark.

The impact on us? We have lost our innocence. We no longer enjoy the ability to move about freely without questioning our safety. We have had to learn about and become part of the criminal justice system. We have had to travel many miles on the same day to attend parole hearings for these offenders. We have to tell our impact statement over and over again. Most importantly, we have had to witness Adam brutalized and suffering.

As parents, our mission in life is to see that our children are safe, well-adjusted, and happy regardless of their age. This assault was an assault on our soul—upending years of devotion and nurturing. In a violent rage, these offenders attempted to destroy everything.

_____

_____

_____

_____

Unit 5. Robbery

What Is Robbery?

Robbery is taking or attempting to take anything of value (actual or perceived) from another person by force or threat of force. Because robbery is face to face, it is considered a violent crime. Victims of robbery—unlike property crime victims—are directly threatened by their offenders. Robbery may be committed with or without a weapon and with or without physical injury. It is not uncommon for victims to be assaulted, to have obscenities shouted at them, or to be threatened with weapons. Robbers may make victims kneel or lie face down; they may tie victims up or lock them in a room—all adding to their fear and anxiety. Violence can easily escalate during a robbery, resulting in serious injury or even murder.

Most victims experience a common emotion during the robbery—fear. Victims report feeling certain that the offender intended to kill them during or after the robbery. Many victims feel guilty because they did not try to prevent the robbery or because they feel somehow responsible for putting themselves in the situation that led to the crime. Many robbery victims suffer severe emotional trauma that changes their lives forever. Victims report that after the robbery they experience fear, anger, shock, inability to sleep, nightmares, inability to return to work, lack of concentration, and guilt.

Why did it escalate to this? Why the gun butt to the head when I gave you everything I had in the till?

—Robbery victim, in response to being physically attacked

Words To Know

- Anxiety
- Armed robbery
- Coercion
- Robbery
- Vulnerability

In the News: Robbery Trends

According to the FBI's Uniform Crime Report, robberies of individuals make up approximately 75 percent of all robberies. The remaining 25 percent are committed against businesses and banks. Review the facts about robbery below. How do these trends make you feel?

- Most robberies in the United States involve a weapon. The most commonly used weapon is a handgun.
- The most common location for a robbery is on the street or highway.
- The average loss per incident is more than $1,000.
- Almost all robberies occur in metropolitan areas.
- The collective cost of robbery in the United States is estimated at more than $500 million per year.
- The average bank robbery nets around $4,000.

Examples of Robbery

Robbery involves taking or attempting to take anything of value from a person or persons by force or threat of force or violence and/or making the victim fearful. The following are four examples of robbery. As you read each story, consider the impact of victimization.

Four teenagers confront Gerald, an elderly man, after he goes to his mailbox. One of the teenagers strikes him in the face, knocking his glasses to the ground and breaking them. They take Gerald's mail, including his Social Security check.

What is the impact on Gerald?

_____

_____

_____

_____

A group of gang members surround Josh, a 15-year-old high school student, as he leaves the campus. They make comments about his jacket and how they would like to have it. Fearing for his safety, he takes off his jacket and gives it to them.

How would you feel if Josh were your brother?

_____

_____

_____

_____

I don't understand what got them to that point . . . to do this to someone. I cannot fathom that.

—Robbery victim

A man who appears high on drugs walks into a fast food restaurant and orders the young counter worker, Sarah, age 17, to give him all of the money in the cash drawer. Sarah gives the robber all the money in the cash register and begs him not to shoot anyone. The gunman shoots her in the chest and leaves with $140.

Who has been affected by this crime and how?

_____

_____

_____

_____

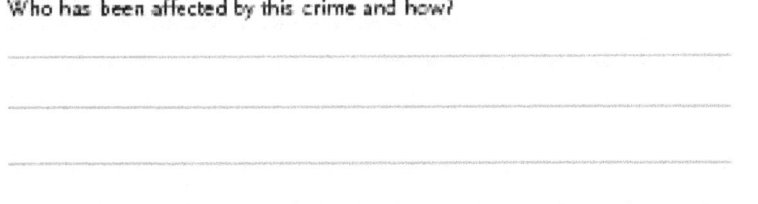

They weren't wearing masks so I assumed they weren't going to leave any witnesses.

—Robbery victim

What Is the Impact of Robbery?

Criminal behaviors such as robbery create a ripple effect throughout several areas in victims' lives: financial, physical, emotional, and religious/spiritual. The following lists outline some examples of how robbery affects financial, physical, emotional, and religious/spiritual areas of victims' lives. Add your own examples below.

Financial
- Property loss
- Insurance deductible
- Replacement and repair costs
- _____
- _____
- _____

Physical
- Knife wounds
- Gunshot wounds
- Death
- _____
- _____
- _____

Emotional
- Fear
- Anger
- Flashbacks
- Vulnerability
- _____
- _____
- _____

Religious/Spiritual
- "Why Me?"
- "Why did this happen?"
- Questioning the goodness of others
- _____
- _____
- _____

Victim Impact: Listen and Learn

After viewing the OVC *Victim Impact: Listen and Learn* DVD clip about robbery, answer the following questions:

What were Jim's reactions?

What were Jim's parents' emotions?

How was Jim harmed?

How does Jim think these offenders should be held accountable for the harm they caused?

 Being Accountable for Your Crimes

Robbery is a violent crime that has a serious financial and emotional impact on its victims. Victims of robbery suffer a loss of security and are left feeling fearful and vulnerable.

No one has the right to commit a violent crime against another person, regardless of the circumstances. Put yourself or your loved ones in the place of a robbery victim and imagine how you would feel.

Which robbery case are you calling me about? I work at a convenience store and I get robbed about 10 times a month!

—Robbery victim

How Can I Be Accountable for My Crimes?

Taking their stuff was only part of the crime for that couple. They had to pay for counseling to try to get over their fear. I will pay my restitution to start making amends.

—T.J.

Thanks to what I did, that lady doesn't trust anybody. Maybe my counselor can help me find the right way to let her know I won't hurt her again.

—Anna

I hurt that kid just so I could take something that belonged to him. How can I make it up to him and his family?

—Jermaine

Additional Activities

Activity B – Bonnie

Bonnie, age 32, is walking to her car in a supermarket parking lot as a car slowly drives by. She is carrying her groceries and purse in one arm and her infant daughter, Katie, in the other. She feels a tug on her purse and thinks that her purse strap got snagged on the car's side view mirror. She turns to see a woman in the car pointing a gun at her as her purse is ripped from her arm.

What may Bonnie specifically experience as a robbery victim?

Financial

* _____
* _____
* _____
* _____
* _____
* _____

Physical

* _____
* _____
* _____
* _____
* _____

Emotional

* _____
* _____
* _____
* _____
* _____
* _____

Religious/Spiritual

* _____
* _____
* _____
* _____
* _____

How would you feel if Bonnie were your mother, sister, aunt, or niece?

_____

_____

_____

_____

Write down some of the difficulties victims may have when interacting with police, medical personnel, employers, and insurance companies. Then read the following story.

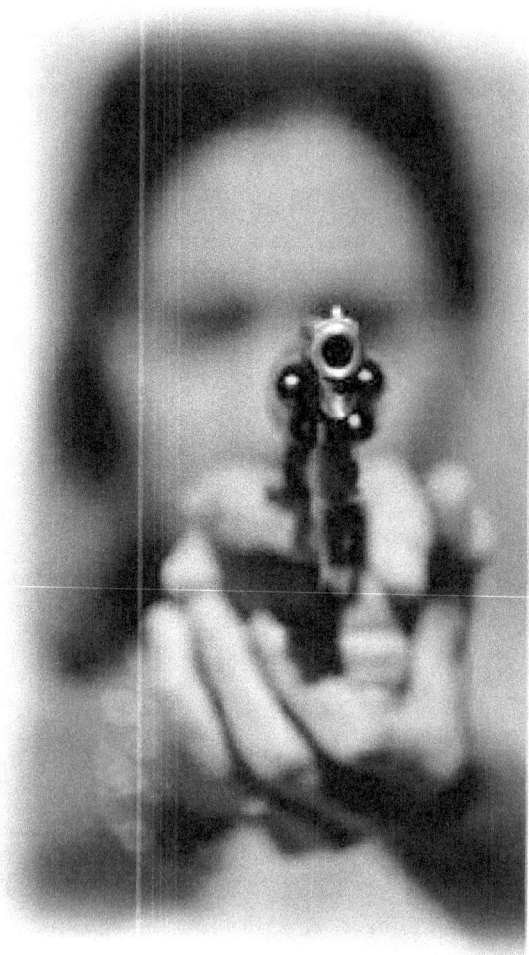

_____

_____

_____

_____

_____

_____

_____

Activity D – Miguel

Miguel has been working at his uncle's convenience store for 2 weeks and is trying hard to please his uncle. His uncle is allowing Miguel to work for him even though Miguel is not a U.S. resident. The store is located in a high-crime area.

Miguel has just helped a customer find his favorite brand of orange juice and is alone in the store. Two men enter the store and walk around for a few minutes. One of the robbers is high on drugs. He points a gun at Miguel's head and the other robber jumps over the counter. Miguel feels a sharp pain in his chest. The robbers yell at Miguel, "Don't hit the alarm and don't try to call the police!"

The man with the gun guards the door while the other robber tries to open the cash register. Miguel inches toward his cell phone on the counter, dials the police, and moves away from the phone. The robbers are unaware the police have been called.

Miguel continues to feel sharp pains in his chest and thinks he is going to have a heart attack. One of the robbers forces Miguel to open the cash register and takes $500. The robber hits Miguel in the head, knocks him unconscious, and both robbers leave the store.

The police take more than 20 minutes to respond. In the meantime, Miguel has had a mild heart attack but is still alive. The emergency personnel take 30 minutes to respond and have to wait to find out which hospital is willing to treat Miguel, who has no insurance. A television news crew happens to be in the area and they begin broadcasting live from the scene. Miguel's uncle and the rest of the family are at home watching the news.

Unit 6. Hate and Bias

What Is Hate and Bias Crime?

Hate and bias crimes are motivated by hostility and prejudice against a person based on his or her race, religion, sexual orientation, disability, or ethnicity/national origin. Most victims of these crimes are targeted because they represent a particular group rather than because of any personal conflict or problem.

A hate or bias crime is not a separate offense. The motivation of the offender is what determines whether the act is considered a hate or bias crime. Crimes include assault, destruction of property (arson, vandalism, or other property crimes), sexual assault, robbery, and homicide. Both the victim and the victim's community are affected by a hate crime.

While most property crimes involve taking something of value from the victim, hate- or bias-motivated property crimes usually destroy value—the offender does not gain financially. The idea instead is to make a statement against this particular person or group. Offenders often target specific places or locations: places of worship; locations of particular importance to a community such as memorials or cemeteries; or organizations and places of business. Attacks on religious and spiritual symbols affect people in more powerful ways than other acts of vandalism.

> *When he was kicking me, I looked up from the ground and all I could see was the hate in his eyes.*
>
> —Hate crime victim

Hate and bias crimes are more likely than any other kind of personal attack to cause serious injury or death. Furthermore, these crimes have many psychological and social consequences that are extremely destructive to the victim, the victim's family, and the community. From the victims' perspective, the crime is very personal: they were targeted because of their appearance or the group with whom they associate. Hate and bias crime victims often fear repeat attacks because their sexual orientation, religion, or national origin is not going to change and may be easily visible.

Victims of hate crimes may stop associating with "like" people because of fear and vulnerability. For example, they may stop worshipping with their faith community; move away from their family, friends, and loved ones; and/or avoid attending social functions with people who share like characteristics. Even people who have not been victimized by hate crimes may feel vulnerable. They, too, may stop associating with "like" people or their community after hearing about a hateful incident.

Words To Know

- Bias
- Ethnicity
- National origin
- Sexual orientation

Commonly Targeted Groups

- Gay, lesbian, bisexual, and transgender individuals
- Religious groups (e.g., Christian, Jewish, Muslim, Hindu)
- National origin (e.g., Africans, Iranians, Americans, Japanese, Mexicans)
- Race/ethnicity (e.g., White, African American, Hispanic American, Asian American, American Indian)
- Disability (e.g., individuals who are deaf and hearing impaired; blind; use a wheelchair, cane, or crutches; or have a cognitive impairment)

In the News: Hate and Bias Crime Trends

Unlike victims of crimes involving financial loss, hate crime victims may not be as likely to report the crime for fear of retaliation or because they don't want to draw attention to the situation. Read the facts below. Imagine that one of these facts affected a family member. How would you feel?

- Most hate and bias crimes are violent crimes against a person (assault, sexual assault, robbery, homicide).
- A large number of victims are targeted because of their race.
- Most hate- and bias-motivated property crimes are acts of destruction/vandalism.

Examples of Hate and Bias Crimes

The Federal Hate Crimes Statistics Act of 1990 defines hate/bias crimes as crimes motivated by "hatred against a victim based on his or her race, religion, sexual orientation, ethnicity, or national origin." The following are five examples of hate and bias crime. As you read each story, consider the impact on the victim.

Vandalism: Race/Ethnicity Bias

In a local Jewish cemetery, many gravestones have been vandalized—swastikas and six-pointed stars have been painted on them in feces and blood.

Who has been affected by the vandalism and how?

_____

_____

_____

They didn't take anything from my store, but the vandalism is too much to repair. I'll have to sell my business.

—Hate and bias crime victim

Vandalism: Sexual Orientation Bias

John and his life partner, Bill, moved into a new neighborhood. Within a few weeks, they came home to find that some of their windows had been broken and anti-gay slurs had been painted on the garage door. The next morning, they found that the tires on one of their vehicles had been slashed. A note was left under the windshield wiper that said they should move out of the neighborhood to "be with your own kind."

How might John and Bill react?

_____

_____

_____

I understand having a different belief, but why destroy our place of worship . . . why do this to people you don't even know?

—Arson victim

Assault: Race/Ethnicity Bias

While waiting for a bus, George, an elderly white man, was confronted by four Hispanic youth who shouted racial slurs and demanded that he get off the bus stop bench so they could sit down. George ignored them and one youth punched him in the head, stomach, and back.

How would you feel if you were George?

_____

_____

_____

_____

I moved to the United States thinking I would be free of religious persecution.

—Hate and bias crime victim

Assault: Age/Disability Bias

Jess, a 75-year-old man, is walking down the street using his white cane that identifies him as having a vision impairment. A group of teens surround him, knock him to the ground, and take his cane.

How might Jess's life change because of the assault?

_____

_____

_____

_____

It was wrong for them to try to kill anyone, but I'm not even gay . . . they just thought I was.

—Attempted murder victim

Homicide/Attempted Murder: Race/Ethnicity Bias

Three 16-year-old members of the Texas white-supremacist group, Confederate Hammer Skins, were out cruising in the predawn hours in search of an African American to kill. They found two African-American men sitting on a flatbed truck enjoying a beer after work. One man was killed with a shotgun blast; his friend was severely injured.

How were the victims and their families affected by this crime?

_____

_____

_____

_____

What Is the Impact of Hate and Bias Crimes?

The following lists outline some examples of how hate and bias crimes affect financial, physical, emotional, and religious/spiritual areas of victims' lives. Add your own examples below.

Financial
- Property loss
- Repairs to property
- Counseling fees
- _____
- _____
- _____

Physical
- Physical injuries
- Stress reactions
- _____
- _____

Emotional
- Sadness
- Suspicion
- Powerlessness
- _____
- _____
- _____

Religious/Spiritual
- Questioning faith
- Challenges to identity and values
- _____
- _____

Victim Impact: Listen and Learn

After viewing the OVC *Victim Impact: Listen and Learn* DVD clip about hate and bias crimes, answer the following questions:

What was the physical impact?

_____

_____

_____

_____

How did the victim's sister, Jee Young Ahn, react emotionally to the attack?

_____

_____

_____

_____

What could these assailants do (or have done) to be held accountable for their crimes?

_____

_____

_____

_____

 ## Being Accountable for Your Crimes

Some people are victimized for no reason other than the color of their skin, their religion, where they were born, or their sexual orientation. Victims of hate and bias crimes suffer serious and long-lasting traumatic stress. Not only is the individual who is personally harmed by these offenses victimized, but everyone in the community is affected. No one has the right to victimize another person or another person's property because of his or her race, religion, gender, sexual orientation, age, or disability.

How Can I Be Accountable for My Crimes?

I preyed on that old man because he was disabled. What if someone did that to my dad?

—Raphael

How would I feel if someone hurt me just because of the way I looked?

—Cassie

Just because the store owner is from a different country doesn't give me the right to trash his place.

—Thomas

Who's to say my religious beliefs are the only right ones? I need to learn respect.

—Mikala

If you were a victim of one of these offenders, what would you want from them?

_____

_____

_____

_____

_____

_____

_____

_____

_____

_____

Additional Activities

Activity A – Hate and Bias Crime

Write indepth answers to the following questions:

How do most victims of hate or bias crimes feel and why?

Who might blame the victim and why?

_____

_____

_____

_____

What extra issues may gay or lesbian victims have to deal with?

_____

_____

_____

_____

What extra issues may noncitizens deal with?

_____

_____

_____

_____

Activity C – Victim Impact Statement

Two weeks ago I received a phone call that my place of worship had been burned down. What a shock! It is extremely difficult to put into words what I think and how I feel.

I still cannot believe that someone would even think about destroying a place of worship, a place where people gather to seek comfort, a place where people come together, where people work on community issues together.

Our place of worship hasn't been in the community for generations, but we have had thousands of ceremonies like weddings, funerals, and social functions. We have, or used to have, a food pantry and clothing closet, daycare, a kids' sports program, and a music program. This was a very special place for individuals and for families. Maybe that's why it was burned down.

There was a lot of vandalism to the inside before the building was set on fire. I was shocked when I saw the damage. Musical instruments were destroyed, religious statues were smashed, and our books were torn up and thrown in a pile.

Beer cans were thrown around. I was devastated when I saw that the old, old stained glass windows were smashed. We all used to love to sit and look at the sunlight streaming through the beautiful windows. We had only been able to afford the windows by having individuals, families, and businesses sponsor a window. A local craftsperson donated his time to make them.

The police say that they don't want to define this as a hate crime just yet. They said they can't arrest someone for hate, that certain laws determine whether this was an actual hate crime. Well, I don't care what the laws say. It is so hateful to destroy the property of others, especially if it is a place where they come to worship and to do good. This is not the first time we have had problems; it's just the first that it's been so bad.

We can't hold services now and there may not be a large enough community space anytime soon. We will have to try to rebuild, but some people have lost faith, and we are all concerned about money. I would like to have faith that a new building will be okay, that our spirit and our presence will make it home again, but I just don't know. I don't know if it will be the same.

I shouldn't be angry or resentful, and we are all working to come to terms with our feelings. The police and insurance people are trying to help, but it was hard to listen to a lecture about how we should have been more careful . . . how we should have had a better alarm . . . why didn't we keep more lights on . . . why did we have rocks in our landscape design that were used to smash the windows . . . why didn't we have a security service.

That was our sanctuary, our safe place! It's a house of worship, not someone's own house or business! Why of all places should we have needed to take all those precautions in our house of worship? Why?

Unit 7. Gang Crime

Words To Know

- Extortion
- Intimidation
- Retaliation
- Victim blaming

What Is Gang Crime?

Gang crime refers to criminal activity committed by individual gang members or a group of gang members. Due to the seriousness of gang violence, many states have included legal "enhancements" for gang behavior. This means that if a crime is determined to be gang influenced or gang related, the offender's sentence can be increased. Gang crime includes, but is not limited to, graffiti, extortion, drug sales, burglary, home invasion, physical assault, sexual assault, and murder.

Victims of gang violence may include—

Non-gang members who are harmed or killed by gangs while in their homes, on the way to work, or attending school.

Business owners who must deal with gang-related property crime and extortion.

Individuals who are or were gang affiliated.

Because of the violent nature of many gangs, whose members often carry weapons, victims of gang violence often suffer severe or fatal injuries, and may face the possibility of having multiple family members and relatives injured or killed by gang crime. Some families bury two or three of their children within a short period of time.

I'm trying to bury my son and there are undercover cops inside and uniform cops outside doing surveillance.

—Mother of gang crime victim

In addition, victims and witnesses often live in the same community as the offender or the offender's gang affiliates. Individual gang members—or the entire gang—can intimidate and retaliate against the victim at the crime scene, during the court process, and upon release once the offender goes on parole or probation.

Victims of gang crime are blamed more often than victims of other crimes. They often are asked, "Why don't you move out of the area?"; "Why did you let your child stay in a gang?"; "Why did you drive through that area of town?"; or "Why didn't you report the first assault?" Blaming victims shifts the responsibility from offenders and creates further trauma for victims.

Gang members often lack empathy for victims or their families. They may continue to flaunt their gang allegiance at the crime scene while being arrested and continue the behavior in court. The media often glamorize or focus on gang members' criminal acts and fail to show the reality of the impact on victims and witnesses.

In the News: Gang Crime Trends

Gang crime is a major problem in our country today. It can have a lasting impact on victims, their families, and communities. Take a look at the information about gang crimes below. Which of these trends doesn't surprise you?

- The amount of money the U.S. Government approves to address gang crimes increases each year.
- Many cities across the country have between 1,000 and 11,000 sites/areas per year that are vandalized by gang graffiti.
- Gang members are more likely to victimize younger people than older people.
- The average cost of a funeral is $8,000.

Examples of Gang Crimes

Gang crime refers to criminal activity committed by gang members, alone or in a group. Murder and extortion (use of fear to compel someone to do something) are just two examples of criminal activities conducted by gangs. As you read each story, consider the impact on victims.

Murder

A female gang member goes along with other gang members she knows, thinking that they're going to have some fun. She doesn't know that the other gang members found out that she has been a police informant. She is stabbed, resulting in her death and the death of her 4-month-old fetus.

What is your reaction?

_____

_____

_____

A former gang member is shot and killed while removing gang graffiti as part of his work with a community program.

How would your family feel if this happened to you?

_____

_____

_____

People tell me I should protect my kids better by moving out of the neighborhood or sending them to a different school. Why does my family have to make changes . . . why doesn't the gang have to change?

—Father of gang crime victim

I buried my first kid in 1988. I buried my 128th yesterday (2004). There is a lethal absence of hope in a community like this. You get more kids planning their funerals than their futures.

—Community gang prevention activist

Extortion

Two gang members, Sasha and Ursula, approach Frank, an ice cream vendor, and tell him that he has to pay them $50 every week if he wants to do any business in their neighborhood.

What is the impact of this crime on Frank?

_____

_____

_____

_____

Me, my kids, their friends,
neighbors, store owners . . .
we're all scared that one of
us will be next.

—Community member

What Is the Impact of Gang Crime?

The following lists outline some examples of how gang crimes affect financial, physical, emotional, and religious/spiritual areas of victims' lives. Add your own examples below.

Financial
- Counseling
- Repairs to property
- _____
- _____
- _____

Physical
- Death
- Paralysis
- Brain damage
- _____
- _____

Emotional
- Fear of retaliation
- Insecurity
- Being labeled "gang related"
- _____
- _____

Religious/Spiritual
- "Why would this happen?"
- "Why would this happen to a good person?"
- _____
- _____

Victim Impact: Listen and Learn

After viewing the *OVC Victim Impact: Listen and Learn DVD* clip about gang violence and gang crimes, answer the following questions:

What was the emotional impact of Anthony's murder on Teri?

_____

_____

_____

How did the impact of Anthony's murder affect Teri physically?

_____

_____

_____

How can gang members demonstrate accountability and remorse for harming or killing others?

_____

_____

_____

_____

We have trouble treating patients in the emergency room when gang members show up when an associate or a rival gang member is brought in.

—Emergency room nurse

 Being Accountable for Your Crimes

Gang crime has a serious physical and emotional impact on victims. Families are subjected to multiple tragedies as parents, children, and relatives are seriously injured and killed. No one has the right to harm or intimidate another person or to destroy their property regardless of the circumstances.

How Can I Be Accountable for My Crimes?

> I feel good that at least I paid my restitution for the victim's funeral expenses.
> —B.C.

> I'm not proud anymore that I killed someone.
> —Shane

> Now I realize that writing my gang name on buildings is disrespecting the owner of the building.
> —Cedric

> I have to think about the fear I caused to people in my neighborhood, people I lived around.
> —Sherry

Additional Activities

Activity A – How Does Gang Crime Affect Its Victims?

Select one of the examples of gang crime on pages 34–35 of your workbook and think about the very specific ways that victims would be affected or harmed. Write your answers in the chart below.

Chosen example:

Financial	Physical
• _____	• _____
• _____	• _____
• _____	• _____
Emotional	**Religious/Spiritual**
• _____	• _____
• _____	• _____
• _____	• _____

Activity C – The Tran Family

Read the following scenario.

When Mr. Tran fled his war-torn country 24 years ago, he vowed he would never pick up a gun again. As a member of this country's Special Forces, he had seen enough killing.

But Friday, Mr. Tran took up a shotgun while trying to defend his family from alleged gang members who had showered his home with 43 bullets. The Tran's house has been shot at five times in 6 months. No one has been injured, but family members are scared they will be killed the next time.

The detective assigned to the case said that the attacks are a feud between two Asian gangs. Tran, who immigrated to the United States in 1984, didn't ask for police help until after the third attack. The detective investigating the case said that this is common and that the shooters know their victims don't usually call police. Tran's children have told police they don't know the shooters' identities, but detectives think that the children aren't telling all that they know. The gangs have been known to retaliate against entire families.

One son was in a gang, but got out after being shot and nearly killed. He moved away from his family. Frightened for the rest of his children's lives, Mr. Tran sent some of his children to live in another city, but they miss their parents and younger siblings, so they come home to visit.

The daughter and some of the other children were home the day of the most recent afternoon attack. A van drove by the house firing shots. The shooting went on so long that Tran's wife screamed at her husband to shoot back. Tran hadn't carried a gun since his vow, but he could no longer ignore the assault raging outside. Too afraid to leave the house, he simply fired two warning blasts into the wall of his kitchen.

He spent $1,000 on a home-security system to help identify the young men he saw cruising his street and laughing at the bullet holes. The police department offered to put Mr. Tran's family up in a hotel after the attack as part of a witness-protection program, but they refused.

The family knows the danger they pose to the rest of the neighborhood, and they are ashamed of how their neighbors may view them. Mr. Tran's daughter cried when describing how she feels. "It hurts," she said, turning her head as she wiped away tears. "We don't want people to think we are bad people."

After the first few shootings, neighbors stopped coming by to check on them, except for one neighbor, who helps fill the bullet holes. "We do not want to live in fear. I am a father. I am working so hard to support my children," he said.

They surrounded me and asked,
"Where are you from?" I didn't
answer, and they shot me.
I'm from another country.
I don't speak English . . .
I didn't understand.
—Attempted murder victim

Activity D – Victim Experiences

Read your assigned scenario and determine what the victim might experience. (The facilitator will assign each group one scenario to discuss.)

A 50-year-old businessman is assaulted by gang members when he attempts to stop them from spraying a local business with graffiti. His briefcase and cell phone are also stolen. He is willing to cooperate fully with law enforcement and is willing to testify in court.

_____

_____

_____

_____

An 18-year-old single mom is raped by two gang members and later threatened by other gang members at her job. She is on probation for a burglary and has been "gang-free" for 2 years.

_____

_____

_____

A gang member is killed in front of his house by a rival gang member. His mother does not speak English, and her other son is 10 years old.

_____

_____

_____

_____

A 5-year-old child is at the park with his aunt, where he is killed during a drive-by shooting. There are many adults and children at the park who may have witnessed the shooting.

_____

_____

_____

_____

Unit 8. Sexual Assault

What Is Sexual Assault?

Sexual assault includes unwanted sexual touching or penetration without consent, such as rape (vaginal intercourse), forced sodomy (anal intercourse), forced oral copulation (oral-genital contact), rape by a foreign object (including a finger), and sexual battery (the unwanted touching of an intimate part of another person for the purpose of sexual arousal).

Sexual assault is not about love, romance, sex, or physical attraction. It is a violent act. The offender's purpose is to exert power and control, to intimidate, humiliate, punish, or force a victim to do something against his or her will. Research has determined that rapists can be categorized into those who release pent-up rage on the victim, those who have the need to exert power and domination, or those who enjoy inflicting harm on the victim.

Victims of sexual assault usually know the offender. The offender may be an intimate partner, family member, friend, neighbor, or coworker. While most reported sexual assault cases involve women as victims, men also are sexually assaulted. Being in a marriage or relationship does not mean that consent for sex is automatically given. People who are married or in relationships can commit rape or be raped.

In 1992, 62 percent of victims were younger than age 18 at the time of their first assault. Years later, that trend has not changed. Young people are still at a higher risk of being raped. Young children, older people, and people with physical and cognitive disabilities are also more vulnerable to being victimized.

Victims of sexual assault who are under the influence of alcohol or other drugs at the time of the assault are unable to give their consent. They may not fully understand what is happening to them or may even be unconscious.

Sexual assault involves physical and nonphysical force. Physical force includes using a weapon, hitting, kicking, choking, or holding someone down. Sometimes, even though force is used, there are no signs of bruising or injuries.

Nonphysical force is called "coercion" and includes verbally threatening a victim into doing something he or she doesn't want to do. If a victim thinks he or she will be in danger by saying "no," this indicates force. Nonphysical force can include the use of peer pressure on a child or teenager.

Some people wonder why the sexual assault victim didn't fight back if what happened was "really" sexual assault. Victims often say that they were confused, "froze" during the assault, or were terrified of angering the offender and causing more force to be used. Victims should not be blamed or questioned if they don't fight back. The sheer trauma of being sexually assaulted can be overwhelming.

Words To Know

- Coercion
- Consent
- Posttraumatic stress disorder (PTSD)
- Rape
- Sex
- Statutory rape
- Voluntary

The emotional and psychological injuries caused by sexual assault can last much longer than physical wounds. Common reactions include—

- Anger.
- Fear.
- Depression.
- Anxiety.
- Mood swings.
- Problems sleeping.
- Becoming less trusting.
- Flashbacks.

In addition, victims of sexual assault often feel betrayed, unsafe, and unsure of whom to tell and whether they will be believed.

Where Do Sexual Assaults Happen?

- Homes.
- School campuses.
- The military.
- The workplace.
- Senior citizen care facilities.
- Anywhere.

Examples of Physical and Nonphysical Force

- Use of a gun.
- Use of a knife.
- Telling someone, "I'll tell your boyfriend."
- Threatening someone, "I'll hurt your kids."
- Telling someone, "I'll break up with you and tell everyone that you're easy."

In the News: Sexual Assault Trends

Take a look at the trends concerning sexual assaults below. Which trend bothers you the most?

- More than half of all rapes occur before the victim is 18 years old.
- Sexual assault victims usually know the offender.
- Both women and men are at risk for being raped.

Examples of Sexual Assault

The following are examples and definitions of sexual assault crimes. As you read each story, consider the impact on victims. Remember: Sexual assault is about violence, coercion, and doing harm. It is not about consensual sex.

Rape

Carnal knowledge of a person against that person's will and with force, or when a person is incapable of giving consent.

After volunteering to take his 60-year-old blind neighbor grocery shopping, the man brings her home, helps her put the groceries away, and then refuses to leave. Instead, he cuts off her clothes, pushes her down on the floor, and rapes her.

Phillip and Maria have been living together for 5 years. When Phillip gets angry, he hits Maria and threatens her. He takes her to their bedroom and forces her to have sex, even though she repeatedly says "No."

What do you think happens to the victims?

_____

_____

_____

My life is divided into two parts: before the rape and after the rape.

—Rape victim

Statutory Rape

Nonforcible sexual intercourse with a person who is under the legal age of consent.

Christina, 14, and David, 22, were casual friends who met 6 months ago at a party. David knew that Christina was underage. They had consensual sex a few times.

Who is affected by this crime and how?

_____

_____

_____

Incest

Nonforcible sexual intercourse between related people who are prohibited from marrying by law.

Jade's mother was cleaning up her daughter's room and found a diary with several disturbing entries, including two that said: "My brother came in the shower with me and touched me," and "He came in my room again last night and told me not to tell."

What are your thoughts about how Jade's family is affected?

_____

_____

_____

How do you use force and power against someone you claim to love? There was no love.

—Rape victim

Fondling

Touching the private body parts of another person for sexual gratification, forcibly or against that person's will. If the victim is unable to give consent because of age or mental incapacity, then fondling may be charged regardless of whether touching was against the person's will.

Terrence was playing video games with his girlfriend's little brother, Keenan. Terrence promised Keenan two new video games for a favor. Keenan did as he was asked and took his pants off. Terrence touched Keenan's penis.

How might Keenan think and feel in response to being fondled?

_____

_____

_____

I don't know how to help my daughter.

—Father of rape victim

Leticia went to a party with her brother and drank half a beer and ate a plate of food. She didn't know that Carlos had been watching her for a while. When she wasn't looking, he put a drug in her beer. Leticia didn't quite pass out, but she couldn't talk or move very well. All she remembers is Carlos touching her vagina and breasts through her clothes.

How would you feel if Leticia were your daughter or sister?

_____

_____

_____

_____

What Is the Impact of Sexual Assault?

The following lists outline some examples of how sexual assault affects financial, physical, emotional, and religious/ spiritual areas of victims' lives. Add your own examples below.

Financial

- Hospital emergency room bills
- Ongoing medical bills
- Counseling bills
- _____
- _____
- _____

Physical

- Problems sleeping
- Sexually transmitted diseases
- Pregnancy
- _____
- _____
- _____

Emotional

- Shock
- Denial
- Fear
- Shame
- _____
- _____
- _____

Religious/Spiritual

- Glad to have survived the experience
- Wishing they had died
- _____
- _____
- _____

Victim Impact: Listen and Learn

After viewing the OVC *Victim Impact: Listen and Learn* DVD clip about rape/sexual assault, answer the following questions:

What was the emotional impact of the rape on Debbie?

_____

_____

_____

_____

What was the physical impact of the rape on Debbie?

_____

_____

_____

_____

What was the "domino effect" of Debbie's rape on her family?

_____

_____

_____

_____

Being Accountable for Your Crimes

Sexual assault victims/survivors may never regain the sense of confidence, self-worth, or dignity they once had. No one has the right to sexually assault someone, regardless of the circumstances. No one has the right to harm another person.

How Can I Be Accountable for My Crimes?

What if my sister was raped?

—Dmitri

I knew she was under-age and I took advantage of it.

—Bradley

Just because we were on a date didn't mean she owed me anything.

—Aaron

The trauma I inflicted on her must have been awful. How can I start to make it right?

—Calvin

I need to take responsibility for what I did to him.

—Jaclyn

What can these offenders do to show that they are changing their thoughts and behavior?

_____

_____

_____

_____

_____

_____

_____

_____

_____

Additional Activities

Activity B – Susan

How might Susan be affected in each of the following situations?

Assault

Susan is walking to a mall to go shopping and takes a shortcut through an alley. As she nears the end of the alley, a man attacks her. He grabs her, throws her to the ground, hits her in the face, and steals her purse.

_____

_____

_____

Will she report this to the police?   ❑Yes   ❑No

Rape

Susan is walking to a mall to go shopping and takes a shortcut through an alley. As she nears the end of the alley, a man attacks her. He grabs her, throws her to the ground, hits her in the face, and rapes her.

_____

_____

_____

Will she report this to the police?   ❑Yes   ❑No

Acquaintance Rape

Susan is out on a date with her boyfriend. He kisses her and Susan kisses him back. He begins to remove her clothing and she responds with "No!" and struggles with him. He refuses to stop and rapes her.

_____

_____

_____

Will she report this to the police?   ❑Yes   ❑No

Sex

Susan is out on a date with her boyfriend. They talk about whether they are both ready to have a physically intimate relationship with each other and agree that they are. At the end of the evening, they decide to spend the night together and have sex.

_____

_____

_____

Will she report this to the police?   ☐Yes   ☐No

Are the emotions the same or different in each situation? How do you account for similarities or differences?

_____

_____

_____

_____

Define "rape."

_____

_____

_____

_____

How does society's attitude about sexual assault affect a rape victim?

_____

_____

_____

_____

What is the difference between "giving consent" and "cooperating" in this context?

_____

_____

_____

_____

Activity C – Mrs. Johnson

Mrs. Johnson, age 72, lives with her 76-year-old husband. Both Mr. and Mrs. Johnson are retired. Mr. Johnson has gone to the Laundromat. Mrs. Johnson answers the door and a stranger asks her if she has any yard work for him. Mrs. Johnson tells him that she doesn't.

As Mrs. Johnson is closing the door the man pushes his way in, knocking her to the floor. He kicks her and demands money. Mrs. Johnson begs the man not to hurt her and tells him all of her money is in her purse. The man becomes angry when he discovers only $13 and tells Mrs. Johnson he is going to teach her a lesson for insulting him. The man beats and rapes Mrs. Johnson.

What is the impact on Mrs. Johnson?

_____

_____

_____

_____

Who else has been victimized? How do you think those people feel?

_____

_____

_____

_____

Do you think the man would have raped Mrs. Johnson if she had given him more money?

❏ Yes   ❏ No

If Mrs. Johnson was your grandmother, would you be embarrassed to talk to her about what happened?

❏ Yes   ❏ No. . .Why or why not?

_____

_____

_____

_____

What do you think Mr. and Mrs. Johnson's family and friends can do to help?

_____

_____

_____

_____

Who else can help?

_____

_____

_____

_____

Activity D – Andre

Andre, 17, was kidnapped by a man, taken to an abandoned building, and tied up. He was sexually assaulted and lost consciousness. When he regained consciousness, he was in an alley in an unfamiliar area of town.

Will Andre call the police?

☐Yes   ☐No

Will Andre tell his family?

☐Yes   ☐No

Will Andre seek help from a sexual assault center?

☐Yes   ☐No

Imagine you are Andre. What are your thoughts and feelings following the attack? What are you going to do following the attack?

_____

_____

_____

_____

Imagine that Andre is a member of your family. What are your thoughts and feelings after being told of the attack? What are you going to do to assist Andre?

_____

_____

_____

_____

Unit 9. Child Abuse and Neglect

What Is Child Abuse and Neglect?

There are four main types of child maltreatment: physical abuse, child neglect, sexual abuse, and emotional abuse. Although any form of child maltreatment may be found separately, they often occur in combination. Emotional abuse is almost always present when other forms are identified.

Physical abuse is causing physical injury or otherwise harming a child. The parent or caretaker may not have intended to hurt the child; the injury may have resulted instead from excessive discipline or physical punishment. Examples of physical abuse include—

_____

_____

_____

Child neglect is failure to provide for a child's basic needs. Neglect can be divided into three types:

_____

_____

_____

Physical neglect includes—

_____

_____

_____

Educational neglect includes—

_____

_____

_____

Emotional neglect includes—

_____

_____

_____

Words To Know

- Abuse
- Emotional abuse
- Exploitation
- Neglect
- Physical abuse
- Sexual abuse

Sexual abuse includes fondling a child's genitals, intercourse, incest, rape, sodomy, exhibitionism, and commercial exploitation through prostitution or the production of pornographic materials. Many experts believe that child sexual abuse is the most underreported form of child maltreatment.

Emotional abuse (psychological, verbal, or mental) includes acts or omissions by parents or caregivers that have caused, or could cause, the symptoms listed below.

Significant stresses in the lives of parents or caretakers may increase the likelihood of child abuse and neglect. Problems may include social stressors (unemployment, poverty, divorce, death), health crises (family illness, alcohol and other drug abuse in the family), and mental health problems.

In some cases, the acts alone, without any harm evident in the child's behavior or condition, can warrant intervention by child protective services (e.g., practices such as confining a child to a dark closet or a cage). Children who have been abused and/or neglected are harmed physically, behaviorally, and emotionally. For example—

- A neglected child may look undernourished and/or may have sleep disorders or untreated injuries. He or she may beg or steal food, have poor hygiene, or be involved in promiscuity, drugs, or delinquency. As a result, the child may have poor self-esteem, emotional issues, or social problems.
- A physically abused child may have questionable injuries such as bruises, welts, burns, fractures, cuts, or scrapes. As a consequence of the abuse, the child may be uncomfortable with physical contact, frightened of parents or other adults, afraid to go home, or act aggressively or withdrawn.
- Most physical indicators of child sexual abuse are identified through a doctor's examination. Behavior that may signal child sexual abuse includes inappropriate knowledge of sex, highly sexualized play, unexplained fear of a specific person or place, nightmares, or withdrawal. A sexually abused child may have low self-confidence, feel shame or guilt, or appear depressed or anxious.
- Behaviors that indicate emotional abuse include conduct disorders, extreme behaviors, cruelty, and delinquency. Often, an emotionally abused child will experience delays in development.

The consequences of child abuse and neglect can be serious and long term. Abused and neglected children may experience a lifelong pattern of depression, anxiety, low self-esteem, inappropriate or troubled relationships, or a lack of empathy.

I did, but I didn't want to tell. I wanted to, but I didn't want to . . . I was thinking, if I told and he found out, I would be in trouble.

—Sam, 8

In the News: Child Abuse and Neglect Trends

Reports of child abuse and neglect have quadrupled since the 1980s. Court schedules and social work caseloads are filled with instances of this crime. Take a look at the facts below. Which of these trends doesn't surprise you?

- Child abuse is reported, on average, every 10 seconds.
- Nearly one-half of substantiated cases of child abuse and neglect are associated with parental alcohol or drug use.
- Girls are sexually abused more often than boys.
- Boys have a greater risk of emotional neglect and serious injuries than girls.
- Children of single parents are at a higher risk of physical abuse and neglect.

Examples of Child Abuse and Neglect

The following are examples of child abuse and neglect crimes. As you read each story, consider the impact on victims.

Neglect

Failure to provide for a child's basic needs.

Maria's teachers notice that she looks undernourished and is usually hungry when she arrives at school. She has been found sleeping in class and stealing food from the other children's lunch boxes.

What may Maria think and feel because she is neglected?

_____

_____

_____

_____

Physical Abuse

Causing physical injury.

A soccer coach notices that Eric is having trouble walking and running. When the coach asks Eric what's wrong, he says that he accidentally fell down. The coach looks closer and sees strap-shaped welts and bruises on Eric's legs in various stages of healing.

How do you feel about what happened to Eric?

_____

_____

_____

_____

. . . frightened, very frightened
. . . trust me, it's very, very scary.

—Tom, 11

Sexual Abuse

Sexually abusing or exploiting an underage child.

Jimmy's first-grade classmates have complained to the teacher that he showed them his "privates" and tried to pull down their pants when they refused to show him their "privates."

What do you think has happened to Jimmy? Would you want your child in a classroom with Jimmy?

_____

_____

_____

Emotional Abuse

Psychological, verbal, or mental abuse.

Mark is usually a pretty happy 6-year-old. Lately his babysitter has noticed that he appears withdrawn and is very bossy with the other children. One day, Mark grabbed another child, yelled at him, and shoved him to the floor. Mark asked the babysitter not to call his mother because Joe, his mother's new boyfriend, would get angry and hurt his mother.

What might be happening in Mark's life?

_____

_____

_____

_____

It just creeps into every part of your life.

—Belinda, 16

What Is the Impact of Child Abuse and Neglect?

The table on the next page outlines the initial and long-term mental health effects of just one form of child maltreatment: sexual abuse.

Mental Health Effects of Child Sexual Abuse

Initial Effects	Long-Term Effects
• Fear	• Sexual disorders
• Anxiety	• Posttraumatic stress disorder
• Low self-esteem	• Depression
• Depression	• Suicidal ideation and attempts
• Anger and hostility	• Anxiety disorders
• Sexual behavior problems	• Substance use/abuse/dependency
• Aggressive or delinquent behavior	• Physical complaints
• Substance use/abuse/dependency	• Personality disorders
• Impaired social functioning	• Low self-esteem
	• Impaired social relationships
	• Increased vulnerability to other victimizations and traumatic experiences

Source: Dr. Ben Saunders, National Crime Victims' Research and Treatment Center, Medical University of South Carolina.

The following lists outline some examples of how any type of child abuse or neglect can affect the financial, physical, emotional, and religious/spiritual areas of victims' lives. Add your own examples below.

Financial
- Counseling bills
- Parents' wage loss
- _____
- _____
- _____

Physical
- Malnourishment
- Physical injuries
- Impaired brain development
- Suicidal thoughts
- _____
- _____
- _____

Emotional
- Difficulties during adolescence
- Anger and rage
- Anxiety and fears
- _____
- _____
- _____

Religious/Spiritual
- Possible spiritual damage caused by child sexual abuse
- Reevaluate basic values/beliefs
- _____
- _____
- _____

Victim Impact: Listen and Learn

After viewing the OVC *Victim Impact: Listen and Learn* DVD clip about child abuse and neglect, answer the following questions:

What was the emotional impact of the abuse on Nia?

_____

_____

_____

_____

What was the physical impact?

_____

_____

_____

_____

How was her mother affected?

_____

_____

_____

_____

 ## Being Accountable for Your Crimes

No one has the right to abuse or neglect a child. A person who commits a violent or neglectful act against a child must recognize the devastating and often lifelong impact that his or her criminal actions will have.

Offenders can admit wrongdoing; accept personal responsibility; pay restitution to help cover costs related to counseling and medical expenses; and, if desired by the victim's family, apologize for the harm that they caused.

How Can I Be Accountable for My Crimes?

> *How can I justify not taking care of my child—to myself and to him?*
>
> —Lanice

> *I'm ashamed of what I did. I need to work to right my wrongs.*
>
> —Kent

> *My actions hurt the child and her whole family.*
>
> —Russell

> *I am learning to be a better parent.*
>
> —Desmond

How can these offenders specifically demonstrate accountability?

_____

_____

_____

_____

_____

_____

_____

_____

_____

_____

_____

Additional Activities

Activity B – Nia

Answer the following questions after watching Nia talk about being sexually abused as a child.

At what age was Nia sexually abused?

When did she first tell someone about the abuse?

Who abused her?

Was Nia threatened during the abuse?

Nia says that she wishes she had told sooner, but she says, "I just couldn't."
What do you think she means by that?

Is there anything specific that Nia says that makes you stop and think or change your emotions?

_____

_____

_____

Activity C – "Drugs Don't Hurt" Role Play

Drug-related crimes are not victimless. In this role, some of you will be asked to take on the roles of a drug dealer, a pregnant user trying to get drugs from her dealer although she has no money, her toddler, and a "John" looking for a prostitute.

Drug Dealer

Brenda, age 17, is a regular customer of yours. Today she approaches you with her 3-year-old child in tow. The child is crying and carrying an empty water bottle. Brenda has no money and she attempts to get you to "loan" her some drugs. You refuse.

Later she comes back with money and you sell her what she wants. You notice that she is pregnant, but you are more concerned about her young child seeing the drug exchange.

Brenda

You are 17 years old, the mother of a 3-year-old, and in the early stages of pregnancy. You are broke, your child is hungry, and you need drugs. You take your child with you while you try to find your dealer. You attempt to get the dealer to "loan" you drugs until you can get some money. You plead, but he refuses.

You walk down the street with your child and solicit for sex. You get paid and return to the dealer. He will only sell to you when you leave your child out of sight.

"John"

You are in the neighborhood looking for a prostitute. Brenda approaches you with her child. You object to the child being present and tell her to do something with the child first. You notice that she is pregnant but you don't care. You pay her for sex.

Child

You toddle around begging your mother, holding your empty water bottle, crying, and whimpering. You say that you are hungry and you are scared. When your mom leaves you somewhere to prostitute herself, you cry.

Ticket Holders (6)

Each ticket holder gets one ticket, which can be used to stop the role play once to ask a "role-player" a question related to behavior, feelings, thoughts, or values.

Activity D – The Letter

Read the letter below. Then describe your thoughts, feelings, and reactions to this letter as if it had been sent to you.

Dear_____.[Your Name]

I know I usually write you with good news so that I don't add to any of your troubles—being locked up is enough trouble. I know it's hard being away from your family. I don't feel right telling you in a letter, but I thought you should know. Your little girl got hurt and has a cast on her arm. I heard that your ex is hanging around someone who drinks too much and doesn't like kids.

I don't think what happened to your little girl was an accident. Let me know if you want me to do anything.

Take care.

_____

[Write in your family member's/friend's name]

Unit 10. Domestic Violence

What Is Domestic Violence?

Domestic violence is a pattern of coercive (controlling) behaviors people use against their intimate partners. These behaviors may include physical, sexual, emotional/psychological, and financial abuse. Partners may be married or unmarried; heterosexual, gay, or lesbian; or living together, separated, or dating.

Physical assault (hitting, pushing, shoving), sexual abuse (unwanted or forced sexual activity), and stalking are types of domestic violence that involve criminal behavior. Although financial and emotional/psychological abuse are not criminal behaviors, they are forms of abuse and can lead to violence.

Domestic violence is a pattern of behavior that establishes power and control over the victim through fear and intimidation, often including the threat or use of violence. Unlike stranger-to-stranger violence, the threatening or physical violence is repeated against the same victim by the same offender. Patterns of domestic violence vary in frequency and degree of violence. Repeated physical domestic violence is called battering.

Domestic violence may begin with threats, acts of violence witnessed by another person (such as punching a fist through a wall), or damage to objects or pets. Victims may be given a limited amount of money to spend. The offender may tell the victim what clothing the victim is "allowed" to wear, where the victim is "allowed" to go, and who the victim is "allowed" to talk to. Keep in mind that it is illegal to prevent an adult from leaving a room or house.

Domestic violence may escalate to physical behaviors such as restraining, pushing, slapping, and pinching. It may escalate further to include punching, kicking, biting, sexual assault, tripping, and throwing. Finally, the violence may become life threatening and cause serious injury, such as choking or breaking bones—or even death.

Stalking may also be present in a domestic violence situation. This behavior includes following, spying, unwanted calling/writing, accosting, harassing, and threatening. Most state laws include this language: Any person who engages in a course of conduct directed at a specific person that places that person, or their family, in reasonable fear for their safety, is guilty of the crime of stalking (NIJ 1993). The impact on victims includes loss of sleep, weight loss, depression, anxiety, and difficulty concentrating.

Anyone can be a victim. Victims can be of any age, sex, race, culture, religion, education, employment, or marital status. Although both men and women can be abused, most victims are women. Children in homes where there is domestic violence are more likely to be abused and neglected. Most children in these homes know about the violence. Even if a child is not physically harmed, he or she may have emotional and behavioral problems. Long-lasting effects on children include sleep problems, depression, anxiety, low self-esteem, lack of trust, anger, inability to form partnerships, substance abuse, and increased risk of becoming either a victim or an abuser themselves.

Words To Know

- Battering
- Coercive
- Control
- Cycle of violence
- Denial
- Escalation
- Intimate
- Intimidation
- Psychological
- Obstacle
- Stalking
- Tactic

In the News: Domestic Violence Trends

Domestic violence is a growing problem in our country today. It can have a lasting impact on victims and their families. Take a look at the information about domestic violence below. How do these trends make you feel?

- Women make up approximately three-quarters of the victims of homicide by intimate partners.
- Women make up the majority of victims of nonlethal domestic violence.
- Women are victims of intimate partner violence at a rate about five times that of men.
- Domestic violence is most prominent among women ages 16–24.
- For both men and women, divorced or separated persons are subjected to the highest rates of intimate partner victimization, followed by never-married persons.
- Best estimates indicate as many as 1 in 20 women will become targets of stalking behavior at least once during their lifetimes.
- Children of abused mothers are 57 times more likely to be injured during domestic violence incidents compared with children of nonabused mothers.
- Children who witness domestic violence are two-thirds more likely to become perpetrators or victims themselves.
- In homes where partner assault is reported, the risk of child abuse is higher.

The Cycle of Violence

Those who have studied domestic violence believe that it usually occurs in three general stages—referred to as the "cycle of violence." First, the abuser uses words or threats, perhaps humiliation or ridicule. Next, the abuser explodes at some perceived "mistake" by the other person, and the abuser becomes physically violent. Finally, the abuser "cools off," asks forgiveness, and promises that the violence will never occur again. At this point, the victim often gives up on leaving the violent situation or having charges brought against the abuser. Typically, the abuser's rage begins to build again after the reconciliation, and the violent cycle may be repeated.

The Violence Wheel (at right) shows the relationship of physical abuse to other forms of abuse. The wheel was developed after victims described common control tactics abusers used. The center of the wheel represents the intention of all violent tactics: to establish power and control. Each spoke of the wheel represents a particular tactic. The rim of the wheel—which gives it strength and holds it together—is physical abuse.

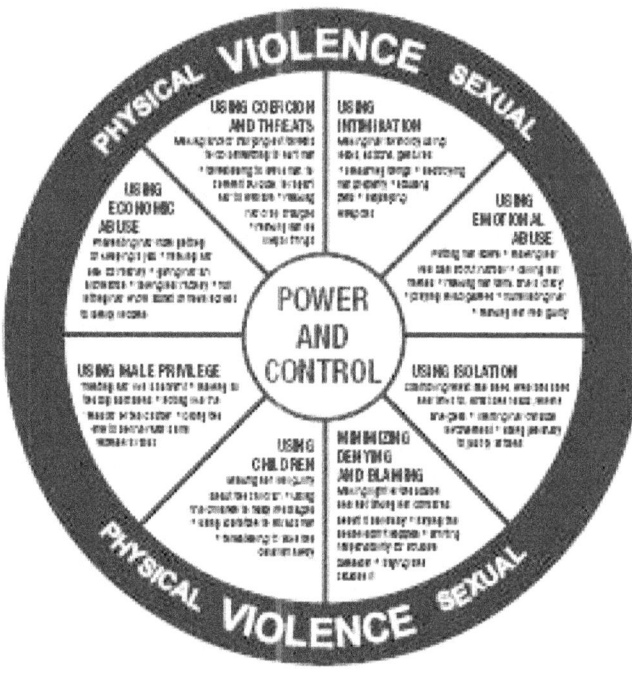

*Created by the Domestic Abuse Intervention Project, 206 West Fourth Street, Duluth, MN 55806; 218–722–4134.

Examples of Domestic Violence

Many definitions of domestic violence are used in civil and criminal law. The following general definition is used in many states: Domestic violence is a pattern of coercive behavior designed to exert power and control over a person in an intimate relationship through the use of intimidating, threatening, harmful, or harassing behavior. This definition recognizes that domestic violence includes multiple forms of abuse—physical, sexual, emotional/psychological, and economic. The following examples show different types of domestic abuse, some of which are crimes and some of which are not. As you read each story, consider the impact of the crime on the victims.

Physical Abuse (Attempted Murder)

May include holding down, hair pulling, poking, grabbing, pushing, shoving, locking in or out of the home, subjecting to reckless driving, refusing to help when sick or injured, kicking, biting, hitting, slapping, choking, strangling, burning, throwing or hitting with objects, using a knife or gun.

Buck stabbed Tracey 13 times in the chest, shoulders, neck, and face. As she lay in the backyard in a pool of blood, Buck kicked Tracey's head with his booted foot, ran into the house and snatched up her 2-year-old son, C.J. He then dashed outside, stuck the terrified child in Tracey's face and screamed, "I've killed your rotten mother!" Then, as the police officer at the scene remained frozen in indecision, Buck kicked Tracey's head for a second time. The young mother, her neck broken, lapsed into a coma. She did not wake up for 8 days.

What are some of the physical, emotional, and financial effects of this crime on Tracey's life? How might her son be affected?

_____

_____

_____

_____

Sexual Abuse (Sexual Assault)

May include constant sexual demands, unwanted sexual acts, unwanted and uncomfortable touching, rape or incest, sadistic sexual acts, demeaning sexual remarks, forcing family members to see pornographic materials, wanting sex after abuse, forcing the victim to have sex with others, forcing the victim to become pregnant or have an abortion.

Kristy and Jim had been living together for 4 years. During the past year, Kristy became more and more upset with his drinking and controlling behavior. One night, in a drunken rage, Jim slapped and kicked Kristy. She left and moved in with her parents. Several weeks later, Jim apologized and asked Kristy to dinner at his house with the goal of getting back together. Later that night, after Kristy said she was unwilling to continue their "live-together" relationship, Jim attacked Kristy, stripped off her clothes, and forcefully raped her, all the while insisting, "You know you want me!"

In what ways did Jim harm Kristy?

_____

_____

_____

_____

Emotional/Psychological Abuse

May include yelling, name calling, threatening to hurt or kill, degrading women in general, criticizing appearance, belittling accomplishments, constant blaming, apologizing and making false promises to end the abuse, offering false hope, isolating the victim from others, ridiculing, criticizing, blaming, neglecting physical or emotional needs, ignoring, withholding affection, abusing pets, accusing the victim of having affairs, monitoring conversations, making the victim account for time spent, criticizing friends and family, embarrassing the victim in front of others, undermining the victim's authority with children, constantly calling the victim.

Juanita and Jose have been married for 2 years and recently had their first child. Since the birth, Jose has repeatedly called Juanita names, including "fat pig," "ugly whore," "worthless mother," and other degrading names. Jose told her that she was lucky she was married to him because no one else would want her.

What is your reaction?

_____

_____

_____

_____

The verbal abuse always got worse when my partner was drunk or high. The abuse never got physical, but the cruel words broke my spirit.

—Domestic violence victim

Economic Abuse

May include taking or breaking phones, controlling money/bank accounts, withholding child support, destroying property, taking or disabling the car, taking keys/purse, quitting or losing jobs, running up debts, sabotaging the victim's work or school.

Jean and Nancy are partners who have lived together for the past 8 years. Nancy refuses to allow Jean to work outside the home. All financial matters are controlled by Nancy, and she gives Jean a small weekly allowance for personal items. Jean recently enrolled in college classes so that she could get a "good job" in the future. Upset, Nancy destroyed Jean's college textbooks and ordered her to quit college.

How would you feel if Jean were your sister?

_____

_____

_____

_____

His violent behavior affected me,
our kids, even my coworkers.

—Domestic violence survivor

Impact on Children (Physical Abuse)

May include physical or sexual abuse, emotional neglect, financial neglect, threatening to harm the children, using children as "pawns," trying to get children to "take sides," physically harming the partner in front of the children, degrading and humiliating their partners in front of the children, threatening to or actually cutting off financial support for children in the event that the partner leaves.

Danielle and Michael have been married for 3 years and have a 2-year-old daughter, Maya. One night, Michael came home and was angry because dinner wasn't ready. As Maya looked on, Danielle and Michael argued, Michael got angry and punched Danielle several times in the face. He also kicked her twice in the chest. Watching her mother being attacked, Maya began crying and screaming. Michael picked her up by her hair and threw her to the floor, yelling at her to "shut up!"

What do you think Maya thinks and feels?

_____

_____

_____

_____

Reasons Victims Stay

Many obstacles can prevent a victim from leaving an abusive relationship. Most victims of domestic violence repeatedly attempt to leave the relationship, but return when they cannot overcome the obstacles, which include—

- Economic dependence.
- Fear.
- Isolation.
- Low self-esteem.
- Beliefs about family or marriage.
- Emotional feelings toward the offender.
- Belief that only the victim can stop or help the abuser.
- Thoughts that the abuser will find the victim.
- Lack of options.
- Threats against others.
- Health concerns.

What Is the Impact of Domestic Violence?

The following lists outline some examples of how domestic violence affects financial, physical, emotional, and religious/spiritual areas of victims' lives. Add your own examples below.

People ask me, "Why didn't you leave?" I love that question. Why doesn't anyone ever ask, "Why did he hit you?" What he did was against the law. When a woman stays, she is not breaking the law.

—Domestic violence victim

Financial

- Legal fees
- Inability to care for family
- Poverty
- _____
- _____
- _____

Physical

- Physical injuries
- Problems sleeping
- Loss of life
- _____
- _____
- _____

Emotional

- Vulnerability
- Suicidal feelings
- Loss of self-respect
- Panic attacks
- Inability to meet emotional needs of children
- _____
- _____
- _____

Religious/Spiritual

- "Why would this happen to a good person?"
- Won't leave relationship for religious reasons
- Marriage is for "better or worse"
- _____
- _____
- _____

Victim Impact: Listen and Learn

After viewing the OVC *Victim Impact: Listen and Learn* DVD clip about domestic violence, answer the following questions:

What was the emotional and physical impact of domestic violence on Rebel?

_____

_____

_____

_____

Domestic violence is a crime that escalates in severity and violence. What did Rebel feel was the turning point in the relationship when she knew she had to leave?

_____

_____

_____

_____

How did domestic violence affect Rebel's relationship with her family and friends?

_____

_____

_____

_____

Being Accountable for Your Crimes

Domestic violence has serious physical, emotional/psychological, and financial effects on its victims. The physical injuries can be severe, and they usually get worse over time. Some domestic violence episodes end in homicide. Domestic violence often comes from a person the victim trusts. Feeling betrayed may cause more pain than the physical injuries. The victim's sense of control and trust has been harmed, leaving her or him feeling very vulnerable. The experience of violence makes it difficult for victims to have healthy relationships with others. In addition, many victims are financially dependent on their abusive partners, and if they leave, sometimes with children, they have little financial support.

No one, regardless of the circumstances, has the right to use violence or abuse to control, intimidate, or harm another person.

How Can I Be Accountable for My Crimes?

> I treated her like she was my property. I don't have any right to do that.
>
> —Vince

> I scared my girl-friend in front of our kid. Saying I was sorry wasn't enough.
>
> —Jean

> I now know it starts with me yelling. I have to control my anger.
>
> —Patrick

> I told her it would never happen again . . . but it did. I have to mean it when I say it.
>
> —Perry

Additional Activities

Activity B – Violence Wheel

Refer to the Violence Wheel on page 64 of your workbooks. Write one or two sentences that demonstrate a specific example of each of the power and control tactics illustrated on the wheel. Also, write about how a victim might feel when the tactic is used.

Sample

Tactic: Using isolation

Example: The victim is dropped off at work and picked up every day. She is not allowed to drive herself to work or ride with anyone.

Victim's Feelings: Powerless, alone

Tactic: _____

Example: _____

Victim's Feelings: _____

Tactic: _____

Example: _____

Victim's Feelings: _____

Tactic: _____

Example: _____

Victim's Feelings: _____

Tactic: _____

Example: _____

Victim's Feelings: _____

Tactic: _____

Example: _____

Victim's Feelings: _____

Tactic: _____

Example: _____

Victim's Feelings: _____

Tactic: _____

Example: _____

Victim's Feelings: _____

Tactic: _____

Example: _____

Victim's Feelings: _____

Activity C – Cycle of Violence

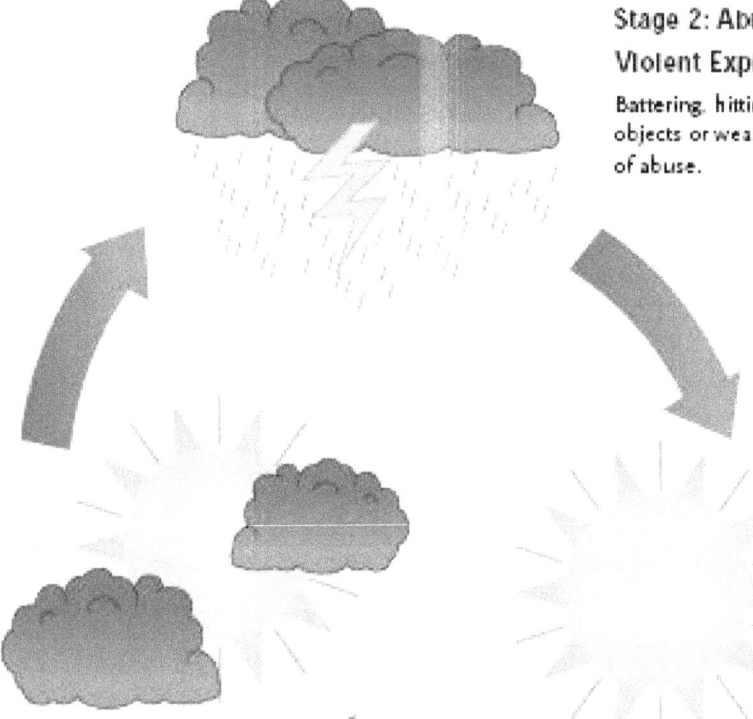

Stage 2: Abusive Incident/ Violent Explosion

Battering, hitting, slapping, kicking, choking, use of objects or weapons. Sexual abuse. Verbal threats of abuse.

Stage 3: Honeymoon Period

Calm stage (length of this stage may decrease over time). Denial of violence, saying they are sorry, promising it will never happen again.

With time, the cycle will occur more frequently and the abuse during the violent episode will become more severe. The cycle stops only if the perpetrator gets counseling and learns alternatives to being violent, if the victim leaves the relationship, or if the victim is killed.

Stage 1: Tension Building

Increased tension, anger, blaming, arguing.

What are some examples of how the batterer acts during each of the three stages?

_____

_____

What is the victim going through physically and emotionally during each stage?

_____

_____

If any children are present in the home, what are they going though physically and emotionally during each stage?

_____

_____

Unit 11. Drunk and Impaired Driving

Words To Know

- Accident
- BAC
- Crash
- Homicide
- Impaired
- Manslaughter
- Negligent homicide
- Secondary victim/covictim
- Under the influence

What Is Drunk and Impaired Driving?

Driving while drunk or otherwise impaired (using illegal drugs or taking certain prescription medications) is not an "accident"; it is against the law. It is a crime that too often results in serious injury or death. Drunk or impaired drivers seldom plan to injure or kill people. However, while they may not plan to cause a crash, they are making a choice.

It is painful for victims/survivors when the courts, media, and sometimes friends refer to the crash as an "accident" or a "nonviolent" crime. Victims/survivors have a difficult time understanding how someone would make the choice to drive a vehicle when his or her reaction time and decisionmaking are affected. For survivors there is no time to prepare, to adjust to the idea that the victim is dead, or to prepare for the feelings of loss. Many survivors talk about not having had the opportunity to say "good-bye," or "I love you," or anything else they may have wanted or needed to say. Survivors also have to face seeing or imagining the damage to their loved one's body from a violent and fatal crash.

Victims may suffer—

Property damage: Drunk drivers may not always kill a person, but they create victims by crashing into vehicles, homes, businesses, or other property. Victims may come close to being injured when the crash occurs. Victims also may have to repair or replace their property.

Injuries: Victims of drunk or impaired drivers often require hospitalization, physical rehabilitation, or long periods of recovery. Some may never recover, requiring home care or assistance for life. In addition, victims may be unable to work and often suffer serious financial challenges.

Death: Victims may die instantly, while en route to the hospital, or later as a result of their serious injuries.

In the News: Drunk and Impaired Driving Trends

People who drive in a drunk or impaired condition create a major problem in our country today. Take a look at the facts about drunk and impaired driving below. Which statements might affect your family?

- Vehicular homicide is the most frequent form of murder in America.
- At any time, there are 10 impaired drivers that share the road with you.
- Drivers with a prior DUI offense have a much higher likelihood of being in a fatal crash.
- More than 17,000 Americans die each year in alcohol-related crashes, and 600,000 Americans are injured.
- Three out of every 10 Americans face the possibility of being directly involved in an alcohol-related traffic crash during their lifetime.

Examples of Drunk and Impaired Driving

As you read each story, consider the impact of the crime on the victims and their families.

Drunk Driving

Eight-year-old Jose had just finished his Christmas shopping. Jose and his family were walking back to their car when a drunk driver drove onto the sidewalk and killed him.

How are Jose's family members affected by his death?

_____

_____

_____

When someone you love becomes a memory, the memory becomes a treasure.

—Father of son killed by a drunk driver

Alcohol and Drugs

Mark and Carol spent the evening at a party with friends. They drank alcohol and smoked marijuana. While driving home, Mark lost control of the vehicle and crashed into a tree. Mark was not injured. Carol suffered a spinal injury that paralyzed her for life.

How do you think Mark feels? How might Carol's life change?

_____

_____

_____

_____

The price we pay for education and prevention is far less than the price we pay for tragedy.

—Victim of a drunk driver

What Is the Impact of Drunk and Impaired Driving?

The following lists outline some examples of how drunk and impaired driving affects financial, physical, emotional, and religious/spiritual areas of victims' lives. Add your own examples below.

Financial

- Funeral/burial expenses
- Medical bills (hospital, doctor, medical equipment, home care services, rehabilitation center)
- Repair/replacement of damaged vehicle
- _____
- _____
- _____

Physical

- Broken bones
- Injury to organs
- Amnesia
- Burns/scarring
- _____
- _____
- _____

Emotional

- Depression
- Denial
- Living with limitations
- Grief
- Panic attacks/night terrors
- Posttraumatic stress disorder
- _____
- _____
- _____

Religious/Spiritual

- Feeling punished
- "Why me?"
- _____
- _____
- _____

Victim Impact: Listen and Learn

After viewing the OVC *Victim Impact: Listen and Learn* DVD clip about drunk and impaired driving, answer the following questions:

What was the physical impact on Cindi's daughter Laura?

_____

_____

_____

_____

How did this crash and crime affect Cindi?

_____

_____

_____

_____

You don't have the right to take a life or change a life.

—Sister of a victim of drunk driving

 ## Being Accountable for Your Crimes

Victims of drunk or impaired driving crashes suffer physically, emotionally, financially, and religiously/spiritually. Their lives are often changed in such a way that many never fully recover. For those who are killed, their families will always mourn the loss. All drunk and impaired driving crashes are preventable. No one has the right to drive drunk or impaired and risk injuring or killing others.

How Can I Be Accountable for My Crimes?

The judge is ordering substance abuse classes while I'm locked up, and I need the help. I'm going to attend the classes and change my ways.

—Kenny

I was wrong and selfish to think, "I only have three blocks to go." I finally realize that I did make a choice and I hurt at least three people.

—Hannah

This isn't the first time . . . but this time I killed my own friend who was riding with me. I commit not to drink and drive. I want to make amends to my friend's family and to my family.

—Bruce

When I am released on parole and I'm allowed to drink again, even if I have one beer, I'll call someone for a ride. That's a good decision.

—Susan

In addition to these statements, what else could offenders do to demonstrate accountability?

_____

_____

_____

_____

Additional Activities

Activity B – Gregory

Read the following scenario and fill in the impact chart below for each person.

Gregory is a well-known lawyer and is interested in becoming a judge. He has been drinking heavily at a bar for a few hours with friends. His friends laugh when he slurs his words, stumbles around, and says, "Sure hope I don't mess up my car on the way home."

While driving home, Gregory crashes into three cars injuring the following people: Karen, a single mom, has wrist injuries; her young child is uninjured. Marcus is married, has a family, and has just gotten a new job with a good salary. He is in a coma and medical personnel are unsure of the extent of his injuries. Tamara has a broken leg. She is a defense attorney scheduled for a final day in court for a death penalty case.

Karen, a single mom, has wrist injuries; her young child is uninjured.

Financial	Physical
• _____	• _____
• _____	• _____
• _____	• _____
Emotional	**Religious/Spiritual**
• _____	• _____
• _____	• _____
• _____	• _____

Marcus is married, has a family, and has just gotten a new job with a good salary. He is in a coma and medical personnel are unsure of the extent of his injuries.

Financial

* _____
* _____
* _____

Physical

* _____
* _____
* _____

Emotional

* _____
* _____
* _____

Religious/Spiritual

* _____
* _____
* _____

Tamara has a broken leg. She is a defense attorney scheduled for a final day in court for a death penalty case.

Financial

* _____
* _____
* _____

Physical

* _____
* _____
* _____

Emotional

* _____
* _____
* _____

Religious/Spiritual

* _____
* _____
* _____

Activity C – "Bud" Role Play

Driving drunk or impaired has consequences. In this role play, participants are asked to take on the roles of "Bud," a drunk driver; his friend Mike; Bud's 6-year-old son; his mother; and an emergency room doctor. The facilitator may also assign two optional parts: a talk show host and the CEO of a beer company.

Bud (drunk driver)

You pick up your son Buddy at your mom's house. You have just come from a party where you have been drinking for about 2 hours. You are in a hurry to pick up Buddy and drive home, a few miles away. Your mom tells you not to drive home, but you don't listen. You put Buddy in the car seat and drive off. You then call your mom on the car phone to prove everything is okay. You talk to her for a second before saying, "Oh, no!" and crashing the car. You end up semiconscious in the emergency room, asking for Buddy.

Mike (Bud's friend)

You are at the same party as Bud. You see him leave the party and you know he's drunk but you don't say anything. You argue with yourself about whether to try to stop him. "Man, he's my friend. I should stop him. He may think I'm nagging him. He doesn't have far to drive."

Buddy (Bud's 6-year-old)

You ask "grandma" to drive you home because daddy is acting funny. Neither one of them pay much attention to you. After the crash, you are left sitting outside the emergency room by yourself.

Mom

Bud shows up to pick up his son. You notice that he looks and smells like he has been drinking. You try just a few times to get him not to drive, but he doesn't listen. You have seen him in the same condition before, and he always gets home safely. He calls you later from his car phone telling you that everything is fine. Suddenly, he says "Oh, no!" You hear a crash, and then the line goes dead.

Doc (emergency room doctor)

Bud is brought into the emergency room with injuries. A blood alcohol test shows he is over the legal limit. You see injuries and deaths from drunk driving crashes all the time. You are upset that Bud put his son at risk and you tell him that.

Optional Roles

Dr. Bill (talk show host)

You are conducting a phone interview with Mr. Bucks, CEO of Sudsweiser. You ask him whether his company feels any responsibility for Bud's crash.

Mr. Bucks (CEO of Sudsweiser)

While being interviewed, you deny any responsibility for the crash, saying that you heard the man was talking on the car phone—which caused the crash. "Was he drinking MY product?" you demand. "I'm not responsible for people's drinking habits!"

Unit 12. Homicide

What Is Homicide?

"Homicide" is defined as—

Murder: Killing another person with prior intent to kill that particular victim or anyone who gets in the way and with no legal excuse or authority.

Manslaughter: Killing another person without prior intent to kill.

- Voluntary manslaughter involves killing another person in the heat of passion or while in the act of committing another felony crime.
- Involuntary manslaughter involves killing another person while committing an illegal activity that is not a felony.

Homicide is one of the most traumatic experiences that can happen to a person or family. It is a catastrophic event that is sudden, violent, and final. Victims and survivors (covictims) have no time to prepare for the loss or to say goodbye. No amount of justice, restitution, compassion, or prayer will be enough. Certain events, such as birthdays, anniversaries, and holidays, will always be memory triggers for homicide survivors.

After a homicide—unlike some other crimes—the victim's character and lifestyle are often questioned, as if the homicide was the victim's fault. Survivors of homicide find the criminal justice system confusing, stressful, and painful. Their loved ones are unable to speak for themselves, and many survivors struggle with making sure the victim's life is adequately recognized, remembered, and fairly represented. In addition, survivors often are left asking why their loved ones were killed and whether they suffered. Many survivors never get an answer, which creates additional stress.

We woke up a family of four and went to bed a family of three. A part of our lives was snatched up.

—Homicide survivor

Homicide survivors differ in the way they grieve. The victim's children may believe that the crime is their fault; parents may believe that in the natural order of life, their children should outlive them; and siblings may feel guilt in moving on with their lives. The long-term strain of the trauma can often be too much—marriages break up, children withdraw, family relationships are strained and changed, and friendships deteriorate.

The emotional stress can take a physical toll that leaves survivors struggling with chronic disease. Some turn to alcohol or other drugs to ease their pain. Many times, while the offender may find faith in prison, the victim's family may lose its faith. Homicide also affects people who may not know the victim very well, such as coworkers, classmates, casual acquaintances, or neighbors. Homicide creates a ripple effect; many people feel the impact.

Words To Know

- Covictim
- Homicide
- Homicide survivor
- Murder
- Manslaughter
- Ripple effect
- Survivor reactions

Homicide survivors often must deal with—

- The death notification process.
- Identification of the body.
- Funeral arrangements.
- The media.
- An unsolved case.

In the News: Homicide Trends

Homicide has a far-reaching effect. It affects not only victims, but also survivors, communities, and society. Review the facts below about homicide. Which trend is the most surprising to you?

- There are 7–10 close relatives—not counting significant others, friends, neighbors, or coworkers—for each homicide victim.
- Parents of children who are murdered are twice as likely to develop posttraumatic stress disorder as parents of children who die accidentally or commit suicide.
- Depression is common among surviving family members or friends of homicide victims.
- Most homicide victims killed with a weapon are shot.

Examples of Homicide

Murder is defined as the willful killing of a person. Voluntary manslaughter is defined as the death of a person caused by gross negligence of any individual other than the victim. Involuntary manslaughter is defined as killing a person while committing a nonfelony, such as reckless driving. The following are examples of homicide. As you read each story, consider the impact of the crime on the victims.

The only way I identified his body was by his fingernail biting . . . it was hard.

—Homicide survivor

Murder

Carmen is kidnapped from her job at a convenience store. The cash register is found open and money is missing. The next morning, Carmen's dead body is found in a ditch.

What is your reaction?

_____

_____

_____

Who would think that you would be killed while you were asleep? That was supposed to be the safest place my son could be.

—Mother of homicide victim

Murder (Stalking)

Phil follows his former wife Brenda to and from her job, always staying out of sight. One day while high on drugs, he goes into her office with a gun and fatally shoots her in front of her coworkers.

How might Brenda's killing have affected her coworkers?

_____

_____

_____

Voluntary Manslaughter

A bank robber with a gun becomes nervous when Kendrik, the teller, can't transfer the money into the bag fast enough. The robber nervously shifts the gun in his hand and the gun fires, killing Kendrik.

How would your life be different if Kendrik were your father or brother?

_____

_____

_____

_____

Involuntary Manslaughter

Matt and his friends join a parade of cars on campus celebrating the football victory. Two more friends, Derek and A.J., jump onto the hood of Matt's car shouting and waving. Matt suddenly swerves to miss another car and both young men fall off the hood. A.J. is hit by a car and dies.

Who has been victimized and how?

_____

_____

_____

_____

People don't know what to say to you, so they avoid you like you have a disease.

—Mother of murder victim

What Is the Impact of Homicide?

The following lists outline some examples of how homicide affects financial, physical, emotional, and religious/spiritual areas of homicide survivors' lives. Add your own examples below.

Financial

- Burial costs
- Counseling and medical costs not covered by insurance
- Time off work to attend the trial, appeal, parole hearings
- Loss of income
- _____
- _____
- _____

Physical

- Fatigue
- Stress reactions
- Problems sleeping
- Inability to think, memory problems
- _____
- _____
- _____

Emotional

- Shock, disbelief
- Anger/rage
- Insecurity/intense fear (panic attacks)
- Intense sadness
- Complicated grief, haunted by details of loved one's death
- _____
- _____
- _____

Religious/Spiritual

- "Why would this happen to me?"
- Sense of being "punished" without understanding why
- _____
- _____
- _____

Victim Impact: Listen and Learn

After viewing the OVC *Victim Impact: Listen and Learn* DVD clips about homicide, answer the following questions:

Clip 1: Joey

Peggy's son Joey was killed in an arson crime.

What was the emotional impact of Joey's murder on Peggy?

_____

_____

_____

_____

What was the "domino effect" of Joey's murder on Peggy's family?

_____

_____

_____

_____

How can offenders demonstrate accountability and remorse for killing someone?

_____

_____

_____

_____

Clip 2: Nanette

Myrtle's daughter, Nanette, was murdered.

When Nanette was murdered, what was the emotional impact of this crime on Myrtle?

_____

_____

_____

_____

When a victim/survivor is an elder, how might the impact of the crime be aggravated?

_____

_____

_____

_____

What could Nanette's murderer do to be accountable?

_____

_____

_____

_____

Clip 3: Jill

Amy's sister Jill was raped, tortured, and murdered 8 years ago.

What was the emotional impact of her sister's rape and murder on Amy?

_____

_____

_____

_____

How did the emotional stress of the murder affect Amy physically?

_____

_____

_____

_____

What was the "domino effect" of Jill's murder on Amy's family?

_____

_____

_____

_____

Being Accountable for Your Crimes

Homicide is a crime of choice. It is the direct or indirect decision and behavior to harm a person that results in death, the ultimate loss. The result of this choice has long-term and intense emotional impacts on covictims and survivors. No one has the right to kill another person, regardless of the circumstances.

How Can I Be Accountable for My Crimes?

I will find an acceptable way to apologize for killing someone.

—Adam

I will pay restitution to the victim's family.

—Reggie

When I am released, I will live a crime-free, nonviolent life.

—Sheila

I will learn how I hurt the victim's family, friends, and community through counseling.

—Emmit

How do you think the victims' families would feel hearing these statements?

_____

_____

_____

_____

Additional Activities

Activity A – Reactions to My Murder

Imagine that you have been murdered. Read the following reactions typically experienced by covictims during the first weeks or months after someone they know has been murdered. Choose the reactions that you believe specific family members or friends would have. Write their names under each reaction that applies.

Shock:

Suicidal thoughts:

Denial:

Anger:

Unable to make day-to-day decisions:

Unable to sleep:

Worrying whether you suffered:

Able to make day-to-day decisions:

Thoughts of revenge:

Sadness, missing you:

Having to take medication:

_____

_____

Attending the offenders' hearings or execution:

_____

_____

Constantly thinking about you:

_____

_____

For most survivors, the trauma of your murder would be made worse by the need to make decisions and plans that are very stressful. Write the name of the person who would most likely deal with the following decisions or planning:

Notifying family and friends of your death: _____

Identifying your body: _____

Dealing with the religious or cultural issues your death raises with your family: _____

Informing law enforcement officials or victim services advocates of any religious or cultural taboos or requirements of your family: _____

Making the cremation/funeral/burial arrangements: _____

Reviewing and paying the medical bills: _____

Reviewing and paying the cremation/funeral/burial bills: _____

Dealing with the court process: _____

Activity B – Plan a Funeral

Plan a cremation, burial, ceremony, or memorial by filling out the information below.
Be as specific as you can.

Services and burial costs:

_____

_____

_____

_____

- Burial options:

_____

- Type of casket/urn/container:

_____

- Flowers/decorations:

_____

- Music:

_____

- Photographers/video:

_____

- Program (type of service):

_____

- Obituary:

_____

- Clothing:

_____

- Faith leader, speakers or attendants:

_____

- Reception/refreshments:

_____

Unit 13: Making Amends

Review Definitions

- Amends
- Apology
- Changing behavior
- Community service
- Forgiveness
- Restitution
- Victim contact
- Victim/offender dialogue

You have chosen to do harm in the past. Serving time is legal punishment for crimes committed, but it does *not* remove the responsibility of making amends for the harm you have caused.

It is your choice to try to—

- "Make things right," if possible.
- Treat others, and their property, with respect.
- Practice self-control.
- Make positive choices.

What is your definition of "accountability"? Have your thoughts about accountability changed during the program?

Summary

Which chapter had the most impact on you and why?

How can you change?

Additional Activities

Activity D – Restitution

Using this worksheet, write each out-of-pocket expense your victims had. Then, develop a payment plan based on your current financial situation and your projected financial situation 6 months, 1 year, and 5 years after release from custody.

Total victim restitution obligation: $

Victim's Out-of-Pocket Costs

- $
- $
- $
- $

Current Financial Situation

Income	Source
1. _____	1. _____
2. _____	2. _____
3. _____	3. _____
4. _____	4. _____

Payment plan

Amount per month	Source
1. _____	1. _____
2. _____	2. _____
3. _____	3. _____
4. _____	4. _____

Financial Situation: 6 Months After Release

Income	Source
1. _____	1. _____
2. _____	2. _____
3. _____	3. _____
4. _____	4. _____

Payment plan

Amount per month	Source
1. _____	1. _____
2. _____	2. _____
3. _____	3. _____
4. _____	4. _____

Financial situation: 1 Year After Release

Income	Source
1. _____	1. _____
2. _____	2. _____
3. _____	3. _____
4. _____	4. _____

Payment plan

Amount per month	Source
1. _____	1. _____
2. _____	2. _____
3. _____	3. _____
4. _____	4. _____

Financial situation: 5 Years After Release

Income	Source
1. _____	1. _____
2. _____	2. _____
3. _____	3. _____
4. _____	4. _____

Payment plan

Amount per month	Source
1. _____	1. _____
2. _____	2. _____
3. _____	3. _____
4. _____	4. _____

Activity E – Victimizing Behavior

Victimizing behavior does not stop because you were charged with a crime and either placed on probation or incarcerated. You do not have to wait until you are released back into the community to change your thinking patterns and your behavior.

You continue to be a victimizer if you—

1. Lie.
2. Con.
3. Cheat.
4. Steal.
5. Damage property on purpose.
6. Verbally abuse other offenders.
7. Verbally abuse staff, volunteers, or guests.
8. Physically abuse offenders.
9. Physically abuse staff, volunteers, or guests.
10. Sexually abuse offenders.
11. Sexually abuse staff, volunteers, or guests.
12. Disrupt classes or group sessions.
13. Intimidate others.
14. Verbally threaten others in person, over the phone, or in writing.
15. Set up another person.
16. Blame others for what you did.
17. Label a person in a negative way.
18. Make a weaker person a target.
19. Take advantage of others.
20. Gossip about others.
21. Start problems between others.
22. Encourage someone to harm another person.
23. Fail to be responsible for your behavior when another person is hurt.

Activity F – Victim Empathy

Name: _____

Date: _____

Recall the crime you committed. With this crime in mind, answer the following questions. This exercise will help you consider how your behavior affected your victim(s).

Describe the crime you committed.

_____

_____

Who was your victim? How would you describe him or her?

_____

_____

Did you know the victim before the crime? ☐Yes   ☐No

If yes, how?

_____

_____

What did your crime cost the victim?

_____

_____

Financially?

_____

_____

Emotionally?

_____

_____

What effect do you think this crime had on your victim?

_____

_____

How did your crime affect the victim's family, friends, and community?

_____

_____

How would you feel if the crime had been committed against you?

_____

_____

How would you feel if the crime had been committed against a member of your family?

_____

_____

What do you think should happen to people who commit this type of crime?

_____

_____

Are you paying too much or too little for this crime? Why?

_____

_____

Source: Denver Community Accountability Program

www.ingramcontent.com/pod-product-compliance
Lightning Source LLC
Chambersburg PA
CBHW080311290526
45790CB00005B/1996